Issues In Expressive Arts

◆

Curriculum For Early Childhood

Issues In Expressive Arts

♦

Curriculum For Early Childhood

An Australian Perspective

WENDY SCHILLER

Macquarie University, Australia

GORDON AND BREACH PUBLISHERS
Australia • Canada • China • France • Germany • India • Japan • Luxembourg
Malaysia • The Netherlands • Russia • Singapore • Switzerland

Copyright © 1996 by OPA (Overseas Publishers Association) N.V. Published by license under the Gordon and Breach Publishers imprint.

All rights reserved.

First published 1996
Second printing 1998

No part of this book may be reproduced or utilized in any form, or by any means, electronic or mechanical, including photocopying and recording, or by any information storage or retrieval system, without permission in writing from the publisher. Printed in Singapore.

Amsteldijk 166
1st Floor
1079 LH Amsterdam
The Netherlands

British Library Cataloguing in Publication Data

Issues in expressive arts Curriculum for early childhood:
    an Australian perspective
    1. Arts – Study and teaching (Elementary) 2. Art in eductaion
    3. Education, Elementary – Curricula
    I. Schiller, Wendy
    372.5'043

ISBN 2-919875-21-3

CONTENTS

DI YERBURY
Foreword — 1

WENDY SCHILLER
Preface — 3

WENDY SCHILLER & ANN VEALE
The Arts: The real business of education — 5

KATHLYN GRIFFITH
Young children, the stories they hear and the acculturation process — 15

JENNIFER A. NICHOLLS
New directions in theatre for young people: A report on the recent work of REM Theatre in Sydney — 23

CHRISTINE STEVENSON
The arts curriculum and indigenous art: Hands off or on — a personal view — 31

SUZANNE M. DYER & WENDY SCHILLER
"Not wilting flowers again!" Problem-finding and problem-solving in movement and performance — 47

LOUIE SUTHERS
Introducing young children to live orchestral performance — 55

SUSAN E. ROBERTS
Quality children's television: The case of "Lift Off" — 65

URSULA KOLBE
Co-player and co-artist: New roles for the adult in children's visual arts experiences — 73

KATHLEEN WARREN
Empowering children through drama — 83

MARGARET H. WHITE
Imagination in learning: Learning to imagine — 99

HELEN MARTIN
The role of the early childhood advisor in children's television production — 113

Notes on contributors — 127

CONTENTS

JO TREADGOLD
  Introduction

WENDY SCHILLER
  Preface

WENDY SCHILLER AND VI-ANN
  The Arts: The multi-literacies of childhood

KATHRYN GIBB
  A picture tells... that the story has not the text has told

[illegible author]
  [illegible] Theatre in Boston

CHRISTINE STEVENSON
  [illegible]

[illegible]

VICTORIA SUTTON
  [illegible]

SUSANNE POPE
  [illegible]

IRENA SOU [illegible]

KATHLEEN YAREN

MARGARET H WHITE
  Imagination in learning: Learning to imagine

HELEN McATEE
  [illegible] Children's television productions

  Notes on contributors

Foreword

This is an important and exciting book and it gives me great pleasure to commend it to readers.

The contributions for this book on the arts curriculum for early childhood have the unifying perspective of the Australian experience, yet explore quite different themes from a range of viewpoints. The collection of papers reflects a strong input to this topic from academic staff in the Arts Unit of the Institute of Early Childhood at Macquarie University in Sydney. Set up in 1990, the Arts Unit pursues and promotes arts education research in early childhood settings through workshops, conferences and exhibitions. In 1992, with the support of the Australian Broadcasting Corporation, it mounted a unique exhibition of international children's art consisting of over 100 paintings by children aged 5 to 16 from 11 countries including Russia, Iceland, New Guinea and Zimbabwe.

In 1994, designated by the United Nations as the Year of the Family, the IEC Arts Unit will be involved in hosting the triennial International Dance and the Child Conference at Macquarie University, arranging panel discussions, research papers workshop presentations and performances by adults and children from many countries. The Conference will provide an outstanding opportunity for many members of the international dance community to come to the University and to Sydney to review progress and future directions in this dynamic and expanding medium within the performing arts and arts education.

As adults we often evaluate children's art against our expectations of adult art and thereby squeeze it into a context and shape familiar to us. But rather than rate them by adult standards of good and better, we would do better to see the works for themselves and on their own terms, and in relation to what has preoccupied and influenced the young artists who made them.

This approach to children's art provides us with a marvellous opportunity to celebrate childhood. In contrast to many Asian and European cultures, children in mainstream Australian society, in our traditional practices and lifestyle, are not very visible. We tend in fact to see them not as members of society in their own right, but as future citizens, or in terms of their potential and how far they still have to go before they assume their place in society. We often think of them in terms of what they don't yet know or haven't experienced, rather than what they do know.

Children of course know a great deal and can communicate to us in quite extraordinary ways if we take the trouble to listen and observe. If we do not, the path to alienation can be a very short path for many children, especially those whose lives are spent mainly in our larger and rather impersonal cities.

The tradition of storytelling in Australian Aboriginal culture, where adults pass on to their children the myths and legends of their culture, is a good example of how children absorb and internalise the heart of their culture from the time they are very small. It also brings them into contact with the very old in their society — something many of us miss out on both as children and adults. In some of our newer cultural and ethnic groups in Australia there is also a stronger tradition of this. Our whole culture will, we hope, eventually benefit from this increasing diversity of traditions and attitudes towards children.

What we should be doing is fostering the obvious eagerness of children to explore and understand the world around them, recognising that this is part and parcel of taking responsibility for and nurturing them. We believe the arts have an influential part to play in developing children's capacities to deal with the major changes they will face in the next century in a creative and self-confident spirit.

Professor Di Yerbury
Vice-Chancellor
Macquarie University

Preface

In the quest for making Australia the 'clever country', whose citizens work smarter rather than harder, and against a background of economic rationalism and competence-based education and training, the arts are being marginalised, in the curriculum and in the eyes of the community. Economically, educationally and politically the expressive and performing arts are being debased because the arts curriculum does not always produce functional skills which are observable and measurable against an established set of outcomes.

National curriculum and policy development committees push ahead with their tasks without extensive community consultation, and arts educators feel the pinch of accountability as emphasis on testing and outcomes takes precedence over process at all levels of education. In the face of such a magisterial approach to curriculum policy development, it is imperative to establish a research base for the arts in education and for the international community to become a network in order to disseminate information and findings as well as spark international debate.

This book offers an opportunity to present an Australian perspective on the issues in expressive arts in early childhood education by authors who are researching, teaching and actively involved in the arts as theatre directors, painters, designers, adjudicators, advisers, actors or arts administrators in community organisations at the national and international level.

The articles are unusual in that they cover a wide spectrum of arts areas, including media. They are diverse in that a variety of issues and approaches are canvassed, including;

— the role of the teacher of young children as co-worker, collaborator, guide, facilitator and stage-manager,
— the role of the tertiary educator in early childhood preservice education as this pertains to consideration of

   (a) indigenous art,
   (b) improvisational drama,
   (c) student processes in movement and dance leading to performance,

— the role of the early childhood adviser in national, non-commercial television production for young children,
— a critique of Australia's 10 million TV production 'LIFT OFF' made by the independent organisation the Australian Children's Television Foundation for children 3–8 years and marketed internationally, and elaboration of the national broadcasting standards required for children's TV production in Australia (for commercial TV networks),

- the role of theatre companies and symphony orchestras in experimental programs, for and with, young children, and,
- the value of language and literature in the lives of young children.

Some of the articles explore the issues from a personal perspective (eg. indigenous art, and the role of the early childhood adviser in television) while others present arguments for and against particular practices in early childhood (eg. teacher involvement in children's work). Some discuss processes and program implementation, and one discusses the rights of the child and the internationally-binding Convention on the Rights of the Child which was ratified in 1992.

These articles constitute a stimulating, perhaps even provocative collective look at the arts and young children, which are too often overlooked, or neglected. It is an Australian perspective, but the issues probed and dilemmas discussed will be understood by, and pertinent to, early childhood educators in many countries, where the arts are being marginalised in curriculum.

Wendy Schiller, PhD
Associate Professor
Institute of Early Childhood
Macquarie University, NSW, Australia

The arts: the real business of education

WENDY SCHILLER
Institute of Early Childhood, Macquarie University
and
ANN VEALE
University of South Australia

In the 1990s policy making in education in countries like Australia has been strongly influenced by the depressed economy and prolonged recession. This state of affairs has caused Governments to view education as a means to service the national economic interest. The result is that the arts subjects in the curriculum are clustered together and represent a diminished proportion of a crowded curriculum. Yet major curriculum theorists such as Eisner view the arts as a possible key to educational reform. Also, evidence shows that humans have always used the arts as a means of expression. The authors advocate for the right of children to have experience in each of the creative arts in the curriculum. Three starting points are suggested for including the arts in the basics of education.

Key words: key competencies, clustering of the arts, basics of education, play, guided discovery, transforming

THE CHANGING FACE OF EDUCATION

Young children of the 1990s, as future citizens of the 21st century, face a world of political, economic, social and environmental change. The family unit is under pressure as unemployment of the breadwinner, or the effects of poverty increase the difficulties of parenting. (Edgar, 1987; Meier, Hanson and Olsen, 1991; Connell, & White, 1988). The effects of a depressed economy and a prolonged recession in Australia have meant that more children and families, live at the "margins" in our society (Bernard van Leer Foundation, 1988) because of changed social and economic circumstances.

Government policies target reform of the economy through emphasis on a better trained and more educated workforce which, it is hoped, will make Australia more economically viable. In these circumstances the Government has taken a dominant role in determining a national policy for curriculum in schools. At a time when children are remaining at school for a longer time, the prevailing thrust is for numeracy, literacy, and technology skills. Concern with children developing key competencies is linked to the idea of ensuring their potential employability, to assure Australia of a place as a technologically innovative and productive country (Australian Education Council Report, 1992). Greene (1992: 203) is scathing about a system where people are described as "resources", and changes in education are talked about in terms of economics and productivity, because "... process and choicemaking are being repressed or set aside. Human energies are to be channelled and controlled in the 'national interest'; no longer is there talk of what is not yet, of imagined possibility.... We are all being required to sublimate our private visions and confine ourselves to 'the plain sense of things'."

Porter (1992) and Cairns (1992) postulate that a narrowly focussed model of the competency-based movement and economic rationalism approach implies the notion of a scientific basis but, in fact, no systematic, scientific, research base has been put forward to justify its adoption in Australia as the national approach to schooling. Eisner (1992) argues that a system which exhalts rationality, defines intelligence as logic and emphasises standardisation of educational practices and competencies, actually mitigates against the function of schooling as preparation for life, creates an "antiseptic climate" in schools and results in the curriculum becoming "intellectually debilitating" (Eisner 1992: 55). Apple's (1982) view is that the teachers are rendered powerless in the face of a nationally-developed curriculum which they implement. Thus an economically-dominated orientation affects curriculum for young children from their earliest contact with schooling systems. There is a seepage of school curriculum into programs for preschool children, as there is a notion of preparing children for early success at school.

Pressure is placed on parents too, for children to enrol early in order to succeed in the sports arena. Overall, the move towards a national curriculum for all schools, will have the effect of standardising education as shaped by the dominant political party in Australia.

In these circumstances, curriculum subjects are not all equal. The arts subjects, (including media) are typically clustered together, and represent a diminishing proportion of a crowded curriculum. The effect of this clustering is that the arts are being short-changed. Teachers are forced to adopt an either/or attitude and settle for whichever of the arts areas lies most comfortably with their own inclinations. This means that the arts in the curriculum are at risk of being restricted to a narrow range of options and of being marginalised. The arts are not seen to have direct relevance to contemporary society or a child's future employability and the curriculum reflects that the arts are seen as noncognitive and, therefore, are a low priority in Australian education.

Eisner (1992) says however, that the arts come close to being the key to educational reform because they have much in common with problems encountered in real life in that the problems of life seldom have a single, correct solution, are often subtle and ambiguous and sometimes involve ethical dilemmas. The arts also celebrate imagination, multiple perspectives and personal interpretation. As Oodgeroo Noonuccal (1990: 156), a respected Aboriginal educator, reminds us "... it's the children who will rewrite history, not the adults. The adults are mentally constipated, the children are wide open."

Paradoxically, children themselves demonstrate that the arts are a significant means of expression. It has been shown that even children living in appalling conditions, in extreme poverty and under severe duress, draw pictures and compose poems about their life, hopes and dreams (Cunningham, 1978). Lacking ordinary play materials, they improvise with any materials that are available to them. Thus, children's desire for expression and communication is so strong that it may manifest itself even in life and death situations (Cunningham, 1978). It appears that the ability to communicate is one of the universal and basic human needs.

Recent studies of Aboriginal rock art in Australia have shown that the Aboriginal culture has the longest continuous cultural tradition of cave painting and drawing in the world which dates back for thousands of years (Cribb, 1992). This discovery, together with awareness of these unique, cultural expressions, is significant because it provides evidence that man has always had the urge to use drawing as a means of expression. The fact that the rock artworks have been durable symbols of human expression is lasting proof of the universality of man's need for expression.

INTERNATIONAL RIGHTS, CONCERNS AND PERSPECTIVES

At an international level, many countries have been signatories of the International Convention on the Rights of the Child (November 1989). This was an important step forward that was ten years in the making and several articles in the Convention pertain to education, play, culture and creative activities, specifically Articles 28, 29, 30 and 31. These articles refer respectively to education and the full development of the child's personality, talents, and mental and physical abilities. The Convention also protects the right of the child to rest and leisure, to engage in age-appropriate play and recreational activities. Specifically, the Convention states ". . . Parties shall respect and promote the right of the child to participate freely in cultural life and artistic life and shall encourage the provision of appropriate and equal opportunities for cultural, artistic, recreational and leisure activity" (United Nations Assembly, 1989). Therefore, countries ratifying the Convention will be required to show how they are addressing children's rights in all of the above areas. It is incumbent on Australia as a signatory country to implement its commitment to the Rights of the Child as stated (personal communication from Human Rights Commission, December 9, 1992).

Perhaps it is no coincidence that in the late 80s and early 90s, prominent educators have written about the extent of contemporary pressures on the young child. Among these authors are Millie Almy, Jerome Bruner, David Elkind, and Sharon Kagan. Also, new terms have been coined to express concerns about pressures on children; terms such as "hothousing" (Gallagher and Coche, 1987), "jump starting toddlers" (Zigler in Bowen, 1986) and the "hurried child" (Elkind, 1988). The root of these concerns is the realisation that there has been a drive for accelerated progression through childhood with a consequent, reduced emphasis on play. The irony is that, while there has been growth of research and theory about play and more is known about the significance of play, less play is actually seen in classrooms or on the streets (Kagan 1990, Schiller 1992).

Almy (1985: 20) first addressed a related issue in reference to child development in a letter written to "Young Children" in which she said "... every child is at once a physical, emotional, social and cognitive being ... let's not fall into the trap of neglect for the physical or cognitive, or aesthetic, or spiritual aspects of development". By insisting on personalisation of curriculum and the need to feed a child's imaginative life, Eisner (1982, 1991) bridges the gap between child development and curriculum. As a curriculum theorist he wants to redress what he sees as the over-emphasis on the "basics" and restore the balance of imagination and creativity to the process of curriculum. He sees the arts as the vehicle for doing this. Therefore, Eisner reinforces Silberman's (1973) notion that the arts are not the frills of education but the central core. That is, the curriculum goals need to take equal account of all aspects of a child's development. No one area should have priority, nor should any area be neglected. Almy's (1985) letter is a powerful reminder for teachers preparing young children for life in the twenty-first century, to educate the whole child.

PHASES OF CHANGE FOR THE ARTS AND THE YOUNG CHILD

Philosophers such as Greene (1978) and Merleau-Ponty (1969) maintain that the way things are, can be changed, that vision is educable and has several phases. As Merleau-Ponty (1969: 175) says "vision would be reduced a little if it was not oriented by the intention to see". Seeing means being self aware and being able to understand and interpret what you are looking at, then being able to communicate this understanding. Ashton-Warner (1985) illustrates the same point in a different way. She maintains that the child has two visions, an inner and an outer view. The inner vision involves imagination and ways of expressing thoughts, ideas or feelings, which Ashton-Warner postulates is the more compelling of the two. Therefore, Ashton-Warner (as cited in Cliett, 1985) indicates that awareness and sensitivity to the modes of expression in the arts are included in the first phase for a child's development, and that play is the most suitable approach. It is the teacher's role to "make the connections" for children in the arts.

Bruner takes this idea further by describing the adult role as "scaffolding" for children. By this, Bruner means adults sharing children's accomplishments causing them to reflect on actions and ideas, such as perceiving the links between cause and effect. The adult role is to observe, help, intervene, extend and support as appropriate in children's play (Bruner, 1986; Sylva, 1984). Bruner hypothesises that the scaffolding process is a mechanism for adult participation in children's play and cognition.

On the other hand Ashton-Warner suggests that it is enough to supply the "conditions", that is, for an adult to react spontaneously to children's ideas, and expression in whatever form these take. While there is still speculation about the timing of how and when to intervene in play situations, it is no longer acceptable for an adult to observe, tacitly note and be simply a bystander to children's development (Schiller, 1992). Play and playfulness, helped by adult play partners (Sylva 1984), are shown to be integrating factors.

Paley (1990) has developed a method whereby the teacher accurately records children's stories and sets the scene for children to dramatise their own stories. Paley shows most clearly how a teacher of young children can be both observer and facilitator for children's own thinking, ideas and expression. Paley's work illustrates the first step in "learning to see" through use of children's language, story making and socio-dramatic play. This requires sensitivity, skilled observation and receptiveness to children's way of seeing the world. There has to be an emotional acceptance and commitment to the child's view in order to legitimise and faithfully report their views. The teacher is, in a sense, still an intermediary in the process at this stage.

ENABLING CHILDREN TO DO THINGS THEMSELVES

The next phase is *enabling children to do things themselves*, which requires the teacher to step back and to lead from behind. That is, the teacher structures a situation by choice of resources, level of complexity and balance of activities, and children experiment, construct and reconstruct in this environment. By setting out various stimuli such as a selection of materials for collage construction and puppet making, prop boxes for dramatic play, interesting instruments which invite exploration, or ankle or wrist bells to stimulate dancing and body percussion, the teacher can remain in the background but children can experience "guided discovery" (Wetton 1988) and create structures of their own choice.

A cultural anthropological perspective is presented by Vygotsky (1986) who calls extending the area of play in children's development — the zone of proximal development. In order to interest and challenge a child, the level of the stimuli should be just above the level at which the child is currently working. If the differences are too great, the child's interest will not be sufficiently aroused for a connection to be made and satisfactory completion to be achieved. If the adult intervention facilitates a good "match", (Hunt & Sullivan, 1974), the child's development will be extended.

The next phase in a child learning about the arts is by *having experience in some aspect of each of the creative arts*. Gardner (1983) and associates suggest that intelligence is multi-faceted and depends on interaction with appropriate resources to activate the child's capacity within a particular domain of intelligence. For example, if children have artistic potential but do not have access to art materials and opportunities, they may never realise their talents. Eisner (1991) also advocates that experience with a wide variety of media stimulates and motivates children, as they are less intimidated by the technology of various media than adults. Children also expect complex and high quality technology to be used because they are familiar with the high technical standards of television and video (Australian Children's Television Foundation, 1989). It is important that young children experience a broadbased approach to the expressive arts, before beginning to specialise in any one area. In fact, McLeod argues that "from a broad cultural base the major purpose of schooling is to introduce all students to the symbol systems of our culture and to develop a facility with their use ... in this way culture mediates between personal meaning and social structure" (McLeod 1991: 6).

Children do not seem to differentiate between art forms in the way that adults do. They can use the media to express how they are feeling at a given moment. They use whatever form best suits their purposes and play at that time (Schiller and Veale, 1989). In this way, skilful teachers can use the various art forms to introduce young children to their cultural heritages. For example, indigenous groups often draw in the sand to accompany story telling. These sand drawings can include representation of animal tracks which are then erased and are perhaps replaced by drawings that illustrate diagrammatic forms showing the routes to animal's water holes and then to favourite resting places. Their stories can be carried with people as they travel and are not dependent on manufactured resources. Similarly dances and songs are composed to give form to the stories passed from family to family. Some of the songs, dances and stories are of longing or have a lesson embedded in the text and show how feelings can be embodied and legitimately expressed through various art forms (Oodgeroo Noonuccal, 1990). Through experimentation and opportunities for exploration of themes such as those examples in the Reggio Emilia program in Italy, children can refine, develop and extend their ideas over a period of time. It is easy to limit expectations for what children are capable of achieving. The Reggio Emilia program has successfully shown the world that young children's interest in a topic may last as long as six weeks. In the Reggio Emilia approach, adults provide visual scaffolding for children's artistic expression. This is achieved through the use of photographs of different phases in the children's work while it is in progress, which encourages children to reflect on the processes of artistic expression (Rabbiti, 1991). Again, by transcription of children's language, words are symbols to show feelings and ideas. In this way children develop a vocabulary with which to express complex ideas. As their skills increase, thus opening up the possibilities for expressing ideas, children experience a sense of satisfaction and competence in the arts as a form of personal expression. They also dip freely into dance, drama, language, art and design in finding an appropriate form to give expression to their ideas. *By exposure to other children's art, by seeing artists at work and discussing various performances, exhibitions and media presentations, children begin to an appreciate their own and others work, as well a developing an empathy with other creators and with various forms of expression.* The latter is a fairly sophisticated phase of appreciation because it requires that children see and understand another person's perspective. However, if the arts are regarded as a core part of the curriculum for young children, it is not inconceivable that art could be an everyday event in the educational curriculum (Eisner, 1991).

FACILITATING THE ARTS IN THE CURRICULUM

The following three ways are suggested as a starting point for developing the arts curriculum in a way which includes, rather than excludes, the basics of education. They are; by exploring the possibilities and boundaries within one medium; transforming from one medium to another; and integrating and combining both media and approaches, perception and appreciation of aesthetic qualities in found and man-made objects. These ideas will be developed in the following paragraphs.

Exploring the possibilities of one medium includes skills such as combining, sequencing, reflecting, refining, and constructing. Transforming from one medium to another includes manipulation of visual media to bring into existence new images and objects. Children can work in two and three dimensional forms to make new images as well as experiencing concepts of form, style, and working to the limitations of the material (Australian Education Council Draft Statement on the Arts, 1992). This may involve use of overhead projectors, pin-hole cameras and new technologies including the use of computers.

An everyday happening in any early childhood curriculum is the occurrence of children creating their own stories. Events such as the birth of a new baby, explanation of dreams, accounts of conflicts that occur may form the basis of a story. These stories can be audio-taped, transcribed for later dramatisation or produced in book form for illustration by children. In this way adults can draw on children's own experiences and transform them into a new medium.

Similarly, children paint or draw on a regular basis. It is possible to interpret paintings beyond the "put it on the fridge'" phenomenon, by looking for shades of light and dark in a painting. Swirls, dots, and lines form patterns to be drawn on the floor or for body shapes which can be created alone or in groups. The painting can be read as a musical score to be played by individuals or elaborated upon in a group. Patterns can be reproduced using shells, leaves, or other texturally different objects. Integration in this context, involves a full exploration of the senses and selection of various art forms which are the best means for expression of the children's ideas. Children see learning as a seamless cloth and see no barriers to mixing and matching various threads to make up the weave of their choosing. Thus the kinaesthetic concept of stretch/contract can be explored in movement by the visual lines and mathematical shapes formed by use of elastics, the asymmetry of body curves in contrast to the sharp angles made by the elastics and creation (through use of light) of shadows and reflections.

Finally, it is important for children to be given an opportunity to describe things which are *aesthetically* pleasing to them. It may be the colour and shape of a bird's egg, or the texture of a woven reed basket, the design of a wheel, and the imprint made by an animal such as a lizard scurrying across the sand, or the intricate designs of traditional fabrics. As Greene (1992: 213) says ". . . That, really is the point: to awaken persons to a sense of presentness, to a critical consciousness of what is ordinarily obscured. Without such experiences, we are all caught in conventional constructs in such a fashion that we confuse what we have been taught to see with the necessary and the unalterable."

CONCLUSION

The arts curriculum celebrates diversity rather than conformity, the innovative rather than the stereotypic in translating ideas into forms of expression which can be understood by others. However, qualities such as accuracy, precision, sequencing, and symbolic representation (which are usually associated with concepts of mathematics and science) are also an integral part of the arts curriculum. What the arts have to offer is vision, ingenuity, playfulness and imaginative concepts in construction and technology, which are the elements proposed as being necessary for life beyond the year 2000. These are to be found in the arts just as much as the sciences. Surely then, the arts are the "real business of education" (Silberman, 1973), and an antidote to a curriculum becoming "intellectually debilitating" (Eisner, 1992).

Bibliography

Apple, M.W. (1982) *Education and Power*. London: Ark
Australian Children's Television Foundation. (1989) Lift off — philosophy and objectives. Melbourne: Australian Children's Television Foundation (ACTF)
Australian Education Council. (1992) National Curriculum Statement in the Arts. Draft statement. Canberra
Almy, M. (1985) Letter. *Young children*, July, 20
Ashton-Warner, S. (1985) In B.C. Cliett, Sylvia Ashton-Warner's message for American teachers. *Childhood Education*, Jan/Feb., 207-208
Bernard van Leer Foundation (1988) Children at the margin: a challenge for parents, communities and professionals. Summary Report and Conclusions of the Third Eastern Hemisphere Seminar, 13-20 November, Newcastle, NSW, Australia
Bowen, E. (1986, April 7) Trying to jumpstart toddlers. *Time*
Bruner, J. (1986) *Actual minds, possible worlds*. Cambridge, Mass: Harvard University Press
Cairns, L. (1992) Competency-based evaluation: Nostradamus' nostrum? *The Journal of Teaching Practice*, 12 (1), 1-32
Connell, B., & White, V. (1988) Child Poverty and Education. Conference proceedings. Melbourne: Australian Institute of Family Studies
Cribb, J. (1992, Jan. 25). Our heavy rocks the top art form. *The Australian*
Cunningham, A. (1979) The children of Terezin. Keynote addresses and philosophy papers of the Dance and the Child International Conference, University of Alberta, Canada.
Edgar, D. (1987) The wellbeing of families. *Family Matters*, October, 12-13
Eisner, E.W. (1982) *Cognition and curriculum. A basis for deciding what to teach*. New York: Longman
Eisner, E.W. (1991) *The enlightened eye*. New York: Macmillan
Eisner, E.W. (1992) The misunderstood role of the arts in human development. *Phi Delta Kappan*, November, 54-58
Elkind, D. (1988) *The hurried child: growing up too fast, too soon*. Reading, Mass: Addison-Wesley
Elkind, D. (Ed.) (1991) *Perspectives in early childhood education: growing with young children toward the twenty-first century*. Washington, D.C.: NAEYC
Gallagher, J.M., & Coche, J. (1987) Hothousing: the clinical and educational concerns over pressuring young children. *Early Childhood Research Quarterly*, 2, 3 September, 203-210
Gardner, H. (1983) *Frames of the mind. The theory of multiple intelligences*. New York: Basic Books
Greene, M. (1978) *Landscapes of learning*. New York: Columbia University
Greene, M. (1992) The art of being present: Educating for aesthetic encounters. In K. Weller, & C. Mitchell (Eds.), *What schools can do*. New York: State University of New York Press
Hunt, D.E., & Sullivan, E.V. (1974) *Between psychology and education*. New York: Holt, Rhinehart & Winston
Kagan, S. (1990) Children's play: the journey from theory to practice. In E. Klugman, & S. Smilansky (Eds.), *Children's play and learning perspectives and policy implications*. New York: Teacher's College Press

Klugman, E., & Smilansky, S. (Eds.). (1990) *Children's play and learning perspectives and policy implications*. New York: Teacher's College Press

McLeod, J. (1991) *Arts and the year 2000*. Victoria, Australia: Curriculum Corporation Press

Meier, J., Hanson, M.R., & Olson, L.K. (1991) Physical education and health education in early childhood. In D. Elkind (Ed.), *Perspectives in early childhood education: growing with young children toward the twenty-first century*, 19-34 Washington, D.C.: NAEYC

Merleau-Ponty, M. (1969) *La prose du monde*. Paris: Gallimard

Oodgeroo, Noonuccal. (1990) Writer, poet and educator. In L. Thompson (Ed.), *Aboriginal voices*. Sydney: Simon & Schuster

Paley, V. (1990) *The boy who would be a helicopter*. Cambridge, Mass: Harvard University Press

Porter, P.H. (1992) Some thoughts on the relationship between economic rationalism and competency-based standards for education and training. Unpublished manuscript. University of Queensland, 14th April

Rabitti, G. (1991). Preschool at La Villetta, Reggio Emilia, Italy. Unpublished Master's thesis, Urbana, Illinois

Schiller, W. (1991) Kindergym for young children in the 80's: hothousing, hoax or happening. *Early Child Development and Care*, Vol. 72, 81-91

Schiller, W. (1992) Patterns of adult/child interaction in a preschool gross motor program. Unpublished Ph.D. thesis, Sydney, Australia

Schiller, W., & Veale, A. (1989) An integrated expressive arts program. Canberra: AECA

Silberman, C.E. (1973) *The open classroom reader*. New York: Random House

Sylva, K. (1984) A hard-headed look at the fruits of play. *Early Child Development and Care*, 15, 171-184

United Nations (1989) *The Convention on the Rights of the Child*. (20 November), Paris

Vygotsky, L.S. (1986) *Thought and language*. Cambridge, Mass: MIT Press

Wetton, P. (1988) *Physical education in the nursery and infant school*. London: Croon Helm

Young Children, the Stories they Hear and the Acculturation Process

KATHLYN GRIFFITH

Institute of Early Childhood, Macquarie University

Even in stories for the very young child it is possible to identify an ideological point of view. This article attempts to demonstrate the relationship that exists between the stories children hear and the acculturation process.

Key words: stories, acculturation, young children.

Through its 'art' every society shapes its responses to experience. Across the ages story tellers, as part of that artistic community, have been able to confirm and challenge those patterns of behaving, those ways of seeing and believing, that are important to the way that society as a whole functions. Every society has the need to record what happens in it and to it; to say what it is like to be alive at a certain time; to describe how challenges are met and how choices are made. Because stories are an essential component of the imaginative reconstruction of that material they have become a primary source of communal understanding of who we are and what we are. Story has become one of the rituals that gives meaning and substance to those personal and communal events that control all our lives.

When only a few weeks old children's lives are given shape through literature. Their toes become pigs going about their daily tasks; they become babies rocking in tree tops and they are given rides on cock horses going to Banbury Cross. As they grow older, the sensory responses elicited by nursery rhymes are gradually replaced by more intellectual engagements with texts. These demand more of the child as a member of society and as a member of a family. Survival (*Rosie's Walk*), co-operation (*The Little Red Hen and The Grain of Wheat*), *Mr Gumpy's Motor Car*); independence and growing up (*Peter's Chair*); love and loss (*Hansel and Gretel, John Brown, Rose and the Midnight Cat*), are themes commonly found in literature for young children because they are assumed to be ideas with which children need to come to terms if they are to be functional members of a society.

From a very early age therefore, children are recipients of a cultural shaping process. The literature to which they are exposed reflects not only the personal likes and dislikes of the adult who chooses the material but also many of the prevailing ideologies of the society from which it emerges.

According to Appleyard (1990, p. 13), "ideology may be conceived as part of the context of a story, representing therefore directly or indirectly the values of the author's culture; or it may be more deeply embedded in the formal structures of setting, character, and plot, or it may reside in the learned expectations readers bring to the task of interpreting narrative conventions."

Whatever our personal definition of ideology is, there seems to be little doubt that literature for children is not socially, culturally or ideologically neutral. Literature does "help children acquire knowledge about what the world is like" (Applebee 1978, p. 53). So there is, as Sutherland (1985), Hunt (1984, 1991), Meek (1988), Hollindale (1988) and most recently Stephens (1992) have acknowledged, a complex interaction taking place between children, the literature to which they are exposed, and the society in which they live.

In the introduction to their 1974 anthology *Stories for Under Fives*, Stephen and Sarah Corrin make explicit their belief in the power of early literature experiences in determining attitudes. Quoting Goethe, the Corrins say that by hearing the stories in their collection children will learn "the eternal laws of life" (p. 10).

Two of the stories in this anthology, Ruth Ainsworth's *Learning to Purr* and Hilda Carson's *The Lion Who Couldn't Roar* are examples of literature which not only acculturate children to the way stories are constructed in western society, but also to the way children are expected to behave in that society. While choices in ways of behaving are possible, the tales make it clear that such choices are limited, and these limitations are culturally based. As well, both stories, through the careful selection and ordering of events, illustrate the degrees to which children are expected to be dependent on adults; a dependence that has little to do with the satisfaction of biological needs, but which has a great deal to do with making adults "feel good".

This is explicitly stated at the end of *Learning to Purr* a story about two kittens who have to learn how to recreate the purring sound they remember their mother used to make. The kittens seek advice from various sources but only succeed when they purr in response to being stroked by their new owner. The narrator's point of view is clearly promoted when she confirms the values developed in the story: "And so it was" (p. 31). The listener is in no doubt now that the kittens' behaviour is "correct". They have learned to purr as a result of being cuddled by Mrs Polly. They have become dependent on her, and she on them.

Both of these stories are about survival, about how the individual is defined, about what it is like to be "me" and about how this "self" is expected to function in society. Although children will not use these terms to define the signification of the tales, the notion of how the 'self' is realised is a level of meaning which has cultural significance and which should not be underestimated.

To help convey these culturally based ideas to young children, both texts are told in a very straight forward way, using a pattern of discourse that is probably familiar to the implied reader/listener (the "under fives" of the book's title). The folk-tale-like use of the motifs of the quest (both sets of animals trying to find "a voice" that would define their place in society); the youngest member of the family achieving success (kittens and a "little lion"); and the set of three "tests" the animals have to pass in order to achieve success are significant for the way they manipulate (covertly) the child into accepting the ideologies inherent in both stories.

It is because the stories use elements of discourse common to traditional literature that this is the case. Traditional literature is believed to express universal truth or to have cultural relevance and so the authors of both stories are persuading the listener (perhaps unconsciously) that these stories too are conveying "a set of values and beliefs widely held in the society at large" (Sutherland, 1985, p. 151). And the values these stories convey are believed to be important for children to come to terms with.

The society constructed in the stories is that of the family, but the members of these families are animals. The protagonists are young kittens and a little lion, creatures who are still dependent on others for guidance, warmth and affection. Such a society is recognisable by children because it is the one in which they exist. The use of animals, paradoxically, serves to both distance children from the action and bring them closer to it. By filling in the gaps between their lives and those of the kittens and the little lion, children unconsciously attempt to make a connection between the two. This comes about because of the subject positions constructed by the authors; subject positions which invite identification by the "little" listeners, the implied readers.

In both stories, the protagonists are introduced in simple, but effective, frames which define the nature of their problem and establish the contexts of time and place.

One morning, when the kittens had lived with Mrs Polly for a week, Tip woke up and said sleepily to Pansy, 'Do you remember the nice purring noise mother used to make sometimes?' (*Learning to Purr*, p. 28)

and

Once there was a little lion who lived in the forest with his father and mother. When Father Lion had been out hunting, and roared to let Mother Lion know he was coming home, you could hear him all over the forest. And when Mother Lion roared back, you could hear *her* all over the forest. But the little lion had just a little voice. (*The Lion Who Couldn't Roar* p. 79)

The narrators' points of view about the normality of the emotional and physical contexts of their stories are clear. In *Learning to Purr* the often painful process of separating kittens from their biological mother is referred to, *not* described, in an emotionally neutral way; "One morning, when the kittens had lived with Mrs Polly for a week, ..." (p. 28). That this should or should not happen is not questioned by the narrator, but assumed to be accepted as normal behaviour in this culture. Because it is not raised as an issue it is a clear example of what Sutherland (1985 p. 51) calls "the politics of assent", where "an author's passive, unquestioning acceptance and internalisation of an established ideology ... informs and shapes a literary work." The gap in time between the act of separation and this "one morning" is significant because it is a gap that children often have to fill in for themselves, in real life, as well as in this story. It is also important because it is the memory of that other place and time that evokes the kittens' recollections which become the catalyst for the action that follows. It is also clear that this new context, which they are now accepting, "Tip woke up", (p. 28) is one in which purring is going to be appropriate because that is the link they make between the two contexts.

In *The Lion Who Couldn't Roar* a story about a little lion who had to find his roaring voice, time and place have a different but equally important significance. Despite the misinformation contained in the reference to lions living in a forest, it is the fact that it is a wild, exotic, but "normal" context (for a lion) that matters. The importance of being able to roar is seen in the context of the family (Mother, Father and Uncle Lion all roar all the time), and in the community at large (the need to be heard "all over the forest" p. 19). To survive in this place roaring is not only essential but also part of what being a lion is all about. The fairy tale opening "Once" both connects this story to others children might have heard and also promotes the idea that this is an isolated experience, one that is peculiar to this family. This has the effect of making this storytelling experience a very intimate one, because it suggests that one family's "secrets" are being shared with another family, that of the listener. So the temporal and spatial frameworks, so carefully established in the opening sections of both stories, are essential components of the acculturation processes operating in them. Because the signifiers are at once broad *and* specific, the children are able to locate themselves within the stories' parameters of time and place. "The forest", (a motif common in many folk and fairy tales) while it can be any forest, is a signifier that carries with it certain expectations that are culturally determined: danger, "hunting"; threat, "roared"; suspense, "he went off into the forest, all by himself" (p. 79); wildness, "The trees were very tall and very close together, so that it was dark underneath them . . ." (p. 83). "Once" can be any one time the child wants it to be, but because it is 'once' the children's sympathies are engaged immediately as they feel for *this* "little lion" who has to overcome his unique problem.

In *Learning to Purr* a similar process is operating, as the signifiers are used to draw the children into the action. This time, however, it is the generalised familiarity they convey that manipulates the child into accepting the appropriateness of the action. Although the word "home" is not mentioned, it *is* implied, and children are already constructing a schema about homes and what happens in them and how they are expected to behave there. The paradigmatic choices are important for the way they suggest an emotional ambience in this home in which purring, *not* meowing, scratching or biting (all recognisable kitten-like behaviours), is to be the norm. The words "kitten", "Mrs Polly" (from the child's point of view the song/rhyme Miss Polly had a dolly is possibly an inter-text) "woke up", "sleepily", "nice purring noise" and "mother" all suggest a context in which gentility, calmness and politeness are to be expected. The impact of their choice cannot be ignored. The "One morning" (p. 28) (like the unspecified home) can be any morning children want it to be. So in this story while time and place are not specifically defined and located, they are evoked in a way that makes them recognisable to young children. This signifiers work to generate temporal and spatial familiarity and in doing so draw the child into the events and meaning of the story.

Repetition, the order in which events are revealed, and the nature of these events are also important aspects of the way language is used to acculturate a young audience. The implied listeners of these stories are young children who, because of the nature of their cognitive development, are limited in their ability to process information and to hold it in their minds. In this way they are not unlike the audience of a play who has to hear (and see) information, remember it and define its significance as it happens, and, to a lesser extent, retrospectively. (There is, however, a reader of these stories who can comment on and interpret events for the child. But, generally speaking the action is not interrupted by lengthy explanation.) So, to emphasise important aspects of the stories' signification, both authors use repetition of words and phrases to help the child remember.

In *Learning to Purr*, the words, "sleepily", "politely", "purr", "gently", "try" all suggest a way of behaving that is appropriate for kittens, and children. In *The Lion Who Couldn't Roar* the words and phrases "little lion", "little voice", "roared", "all over the forest", "lost my voice", also give definition to ways of being and behaving that are essential if you are going to survive as a lion and, by implication, as a child.

But authors also manipulate the order in which the listener receives information because they are aware, consciously or unconsciously, of the need to capture the child's attention, hold it *and* convey meaning. This is another reason why the patterning of language evident in many simple animal folk tales is used effectively in both texts. Children are familiar with this type of discourse and so expect to meet animals speaking and acting like humans, events occurring in threes and the ultimate success of the protagonist. There is an expected ordering of such items in the traditional tale and children have already begun to learn about this.

In *Learning to Purr* the kittens' problem is conveyed in the opening paragraph. Their need to purr is linked emotively to memories of their mother; "Do you remember the nice purring noise mother used to make sometimes" (p. 28) But this memory is given further definition by the order of its components, and by placing it in a very particular context which demonstrates how it was used:

"When she was pleased with us"
"Or sorry for us"
"Or wanted us to go to sleep" (p. 28)

"Pleased", "sorry" and "wanted" are the words that matter most in this important triad. They are all words that suggest ways of controlling behaviour and, more specifically, ways mothers control the behaviour of her children. The child has barely settled into the story when this dictum is presented. The meaning, generated by the paradigmatic and syntagmatic choices, could not be more explicit. The ordering of the behaviour is important to consider in more detail. "When she was pleased with us" (p. 28) is likely to be remembered by the child because it is the first statement. Implied in it is the fact that for the mother to be pleased, the kittens must have done something pleasing. It is then a gentle, but nonetheless powerful, way into the story's pattern of action which is based on stimulus and response behaviour. This is especially evident in the climax when the surrogate mother, Mrs Polly, stimulates the kittens by "strok(ing) them with her warm hands and tick(ling) them under their fluffy chins" (p. 30), and they respond by purring!

So purring when being pleased with them carries the weight of meaning because it is the first statement, and because it is the only one of the three that is attributed to a specific kitten, Pansy. The next two statements of untagged dialogue (another example of children having to fill in a gap), while important, are seen as parts of the same 'type' of controlling behaviour. The omitting of the speakers' names supports this.

Similarly, when the kittens set out on their quest, the order in which they confront the three "objects" from whom they "politely" seek advice is important. This time, however, it is the final confrontation that is most significant. They begin by asking a creature that, unlike them, represents freedom and independence, and they end by asking an object that is totally dependent on others to function at all. What is happening here is the kittens trying to establish their role in this new environment; they are working out what they have to do to fulfil their, and others, notion of "self".

The first creature they meet is the bee who, despite being an "animal", is everything they are not. He is bossy and rude; "Purr indeed!" replied the bumble bee crossly. "What rubbish you talk!" (p. 28) and, above all, independent and unable to be tamed "Just then he found the part of the window that was open and he sailed into the sunshine" (p. 29). He is definitely *not* a good model for the kittens, or for children.

The next two objects they turn to are both inanimate, but familiar, items in any well run household. The kettle and the vacuum cleaner, unlike the bee, only function when Mrs Polly intervenes. While the kettle can survive for a time without adult intervention, "I am singing. I always start to sing just when the water inside me is ready to boil. Then Mrs Polly . . ." (p. 29), the vacuum cleaner cannot; "She plugged it into the proper place and began to sweep the rug." . . . "Mrs Polly turned the switch off for a moment and the noise stopped" (p. 30). What is important to recognise here is that it is *this* confrontation with the cleaner that is closest in place and kind to the kittens discovering that they too respond in a totally predictable way when they are "turned on"; "She stroked them with her warm hands and tickled them under their fluffy chins" (p. 30) "I can hear someone purring" said Tip sleepily (p. 31). It is the juxtaposition of these incidents that gives shape to the meaning of the story, and thus helps children make the link between the two.

In *The Lion Who Couldn't Roar*, ordering also controls the way the discourse makes culturally significant statements about the nature of 'self', and about suitable ways of behaving in society. Ordering in terms of the lion's place and size in his family is highlighted throughout. The phrase "*little lion*" is repeated seventeen times, so children listening to the story, cannot fail to appreciate that the problem of this smallest member of the lion family is one which he must overcome despite his size. The power of these creatures, and their position in society as a whole, is also part of this ordering process.

The fact that their roars are heard "all over the forest" (p. 79) suggests that this is the territory over which they have control, and that roaring is a powerful agent in maintaining that control. So unless the little lion is able to fit into this way of behaving he will not fit into society as a whole. It is a powerful cultural message. Unlike the kittens who learn appropriate survival behaviour by staying in the home, the little lion has to move out of the family environment and achieve success "out there", "all by himself" (p. 79). Learning to balance dependence and independence (he has to be rescued by his mother) as opposed to the kittens learning total dependence is what matters here.

Again the order in which his three tasks are organised has relevance for signification of the discourse as a whole. Always polite, the little lion goes first to the "air" of the monkeys who, unlike the little lion, are frivolous, rude and playful. He then moves to the "water" and the hippopotamus who is large, uncaring and unsympathetic. Finally he goes to the "earth" of the snake who pushes him into finding a solution. The first two animals he asks are not of his kind (his element) and so he fails in his quest. But when he comes to the snake who is closest to being able to understand his point of view, he meets with success. The snake, like the lion, is little, (a child?), it lives close to the ground, (the earth), and has the power to threaten other animals. But, most importantly, it has a voice that is almost insignificant (again like that of a child). It is through the actions of this *third* forest creature that the lion achieves his goal by proving that he too can be heard "far way in the forest" (p. 83). The irony is, of course, that his roar is the result of fear, a most un-lion-like response; but a response nonetheless which young children would understand.

Another aspect of the acculturation process which has to be considered is the role of the storyteller (*not* the narrator). Because adults are reading these tales to very young children, those suprasegmental components, essential to any dramatic performance, come into play here as well. Adults reading these tales will embellish the written text with gestures, smiles, nods of approval, changes in tone, volume, stress and intonation, all of which will act as "shapers" of meaning in for the child. While remaining faithful to the written discourse their acceptance of rejection of its meaning apparently innocuous statements like, "That was a good story" or "I'm pleased the kitten/lion learned how to purr/roar" are by way of stamping an adult's imprimatur on the work as a whole.

What emerges in both stories are sets of "desirable values associated with niceness of character" (Hollindale, 1988, p. 21). This is what adults in this society believe young children ought to be exposed to. The search for self and finding a way of behaving that both resolves conflict and satisfies internal emotional needs are limited and shaped by the society in which this quest takes place. Both the kittens and the little lion act in ways that support the status quo. They are, in fact, models of acceptable behaviour for the young children who listen to their adventures. As Stephens states (1992, p. 55) "part of the socialisation of the child is that she learns to operate as a subject within various discourse types." The omniscient narrators of both stories have organised their discourses in ways that invite the children to identify with the protagonists of their respective stories.

What the authors of both stories have done is to recognise and use the power inherent in the conventions of the traditional story to describe and praise the conventions of behaviour in contemporary western society. Stories are powerful shapers of experience and even in literature for the very young, their ideologies "have potential powers of persuasion" (Sutherland, 1985, p. 157).

Through the process of exposure to story, children become part of a literary community, and unknowingly share experiences with other children which society endorses as being valuable. These "intense emotional associations" (Corrin, 1979, p. 9) which society sees as "good", are instrumental in the way they transmit a literary heritage, in the way they provide information about the way society as a whole functions, and about the way individual members of that society are expected to behave. In short, literature is used as a vehicle for acculturation.

References

Applebee, A. (1978) *The Child's Concept of Story*. Chicago: University of Chicago Press
Appleyard, S.J. (1990) *Becoming a Reader. The Experience of Fiction from Childhood to Adolescence*, Cambridge: Cambridge University Press
Corrin, Sarah, & Corrin, Stephen, (1974) *Stories for Under Fives*. London: Puffin Books
Hollindale, Peter (1988) Ideology and the children's book, *Signal*, 55, 3-22
Hunt, Peter (1984) Childish criticism. The subculture of the child, the book and the critic. *Signal*, 42, 42-59
Meek, Margaret (1988) *How Texts Teach What Readers Learn*. London: The Thimble Press
Stephens, John (1992) *Language and Ideology in Children's Fiction*. London: Longmans
Sutherland, Robert, D. (1985) Hidden persuaders: political ideologies in literature for children. *Children's Literature in Education*, 16(3), 143-158

Books Cited

Burningham, J. (1970) *Mr Gumpsy's Outing*. London: Jonathan Cape
Hutchins, P. (1968) *Rosie's Walk*. London: The Bodley Head
Keats, E.J. (1967) *Peter's Chair* London: The Bodley Head

New directions in theatre for young people. A report on the recent work of REM theatre in Sydney

JENNIFER A. NICHOLLS

Institute of Early Childhood, Macquarie University

This paper outlines new directions in Theatre-in-Education/Theatre for Young People by profiling the work of one Company, REM Theatre, based in Sydney. REM's recent production for children was researched in Australia's neighbouring Oceanic island, Fiji. The company exchanged myths, legends, and performance/production techniques with local Fijian villagers and returned to Australia to synthesise their research into a performance suitable for 3-10 year olds. REM's production introduces children to the importance of stories and storytelling by recreating mythical characters and legends from Fijian history. In addition, REM's production techniques involves a carefully constructed process that introduces the audience to the theatricality of the performance, inviting them to identify a range of theatrical concepts and elements. This process of theatrical deconstruction is discussed using comments provided by children who attended the production.

Theatre-in-Education (TIE) companies have been gracing our schools for over a decade. In many countries their growth has been prolific and their charter has been both educative and theatrically innovative. Recently, the Australia Council, (the Federal Government's funding and advisory body), requested that TIE companies reexamine their philosophies and practices. At an invitational seminar attended by some 20 directors, administrators and artists, from the major theatre-in-education companies in Australia, various artistic agendas, issues and concerns were discussed.

From this seminar, one thing was clear; theatre-in-education was in a hiatus. Having been through the phases of didactic, issue-based theatre ranging from child abuse, to peer pressure, to 'how to overcome one's fear of the dark', theatre in education, was, by its own peer pressure, needing to take a new direction, and set fresh agendas.

As a result there is a growing sophistication in the work being produced for children and young people in Australia that addresses all aspects of theatre production, in particular, a reexamination of the very essence or theatricality of performance.

Another result of this important meeting has been a general acknowledgment of a change to the nomenclature, Theatre-In-Education, to Theatre for Young

People (TYP). It was agreed that TYP more accurately described the work of these companies, did not restrict them to perform in school venues alone and meant that they were not subsequently constrained by the school curriculum for performance material. More importantly, it lifted their status from the marginalised "fringe" to "professional theatre" in the eyes of funding bodies, agents, mainstream theatre companies and the general public.

While issues and themes continue to dominate the central mechanism of Theatre for Young People, there is a gradual return to the fundamental elements of theatre and theatre production by companies dedicated to produce quality work for young audiences.

This is exemplified by the work of one company whose work is profiled in this article; that is REM Theatre, who are based in Sydney. Short for Rapid Eye Movement, REM's work centres around storytelling, dreams and myths, acknowledging that the imagination and sub-conscious is at its most active in the seventh stage of sleep referred to as R.E.M. Although REM performs for adults as well as young people, their recent productions have been targeted to the 3–10 age group.

In 1991 REM presented a production to Australian audiences called *Myths and Muses*. In this piece, REM researched myths from many different cultures (Asian, Aboriginal Dreamtime, the Americas, Africa and Europe) and re-created their own dramatic story for children which explained how the world began and provided an explanation for what keeps it going.

Myths and Muses told the story of *Wayan*, the first born, how she was created from clay, how the sun and moon were made and how *Wayan*, in helping the *tall ones*, made life on earth possible and became a human being. On her journey of discovery, *Wayan* encounters a variety of characters and situations drawn from diverse cultural resources.

Within this narrative, young audiences were introduced to the stories and story telling techniques of other cultures, gently reminding them of the need to respect and nurture the world instead of taking it for granted.

REM's second production, *More Myths and Muses*, moves on from the story of the creation of life to fostering an appreciation of the cycle of life and the survival of stories told by our ancestors. The company sets out aims for this particular production which are succinct and challenging, and reflect the growing concern of many TYP companies to introduce audiences to fundamental elements of theatre as follows:

- Give children an understanding of theatre and the roles actors play;
- Help children develop and understanding and appreciation of the stories belonging to the diverse cultures in our society;
- Act as a stimulus for the discovery and discussion of further myths from other parts of the world;
- Introduce Australian audiences to a style of performance which is influenced by Oceanic and Asian modes of storytelling, without elaborate sets; and

- Provide children, teachers and parents with a thought provoking and enjoyable theatrical experience. (*Program Notes*)

In order to create this performance, REM applied to the Australia Council under its Creative Development program to spend two months touring the island of Fiji, in the central Pacific, researching the myths and culture of its people. The application was successful on two grounds. REM has a sound reputation as a leader and innovator of children's theatre in Australia, and second, the increasing cross cultural awareness of Australia, and its desire to forge strong links with its Asian and Pacific neighbours, meant that REM Theatre's planned program of performance and research in Fiji would be an important development in cultural exchange.

REM theatre spent two months living and working in Fiji. The company travelled with their first show, *Myths and Muses* and performed it extensively throughout the island for a variety of audiences and in different venues ranging from the Museum in the capital city, Suva, to the remote village of Bukoya in the western highlands. Of the experience, REM said;

Fiji proved to be a rich environment for both performance and research. Its culture has been influenced by the journeys made by Melanesians and Polynesians as they passed through or near Fiji in the course of many centuries.

Teacher's Resource Booklet

REM was able to experience, at first hand, the telling of traditional stories from village elders. The process as described by actor, and founding member of REM, Roger Rynd, was as follows:

In one village we went to in the highlands I went to see the *Turaga ne ko ro* (executive officer of village). He interviewed me for 40 minutes. He couldn't speak English, but through the schoolteacher acting as translator, he was able to vet me. Questions like — "How many of you are there? What are you going to do? Are you selling religion"

When approval was finally given, a *sevu sevu* (welcoming ceremony) was performed. Not only were we permitted to stay in the village but we stayed in the house of the Tura ne ko ro. His family vacated their sleeping quarters for us and they moved to another part of the house.

R. Rynd, personal communication, March 2nd 1993

From this point REM was invited to perform their play and in turn, the villagers would regale the Australian storytellers with their own myths and stories passed down the generations.

Rynd's story of REM in Fiji continues,

Fijian life revolves around the understanding of *Iyau*; simply all things go round, the giver will eventually receive. When one visits a storyteller one brings an offering or *Nabu*. In fact, many early stories revolve around the competition to produce the finest *Nabu* and thus hear the best story ... Our *Nabu* was our story, it was the best we had and in the way of *Iyau* the whole community were very appreciative and in return gave us a rich resource of stories, recordings and ideas.

On their return to Australia, the company spent three months collating and synthesising the wealth of information they had acquired. The artistic challenge was to simplify that data into a carefully constructed narrative that weaved the elements of text, storytelling, movement, music, and design into the production. The company were adamant that they did not lose the important ambience and influences of the Fijian culture which they had grown to know and appreciate, and as Rynd (1993) states, "Not offend the traditional cultural groups who possess those stories and history"

The result of this intensive workshop and rehearsal process was the creation of More *Myths and Muses*, a highly theatrical and informative production that incorporated the myths and stories of this diverse and rich oceanic culture, but also introduced its audience to the magic and spectacle of theatre.

In this particular story, we once again meet *Wayan*, the first born, and join her search for the serpent deity *Ratu-Mai-Mbula*. We also meet the greedy Puku who has drained the cup of life and consequently caused the death of *Wati-Kutjara*, the Lizard Man. The young audience follow Wayan on her quest as she confronts danger, and encounters friends and foe. It is this quest that becomes the central action of the narrative.

Along the way we meet *Pele*, the fire goddess who inhabits volcanoes and we laugh at the antics of the *Velee* or wood spirits, who do everything back to front, including laughing when they are sad and nodding their heads when they want to say "no".

When *Wayan* eventually reaches the serpent deity, she learns that the cup cannot be refilled. However, he does give her a second cup and with the water from that, a pattern of life will be established: cold winters, warm summers; the sadness of death and the joy of life.

The fundamental elements of storytelling and myth continue in this production. It is the universality of myth and the ability for myth to communicate at all levels that becomes the raison d'etre for REM's production. Also, within the framework of this story, REM gently and intelligently introduces its young audience to a wide range of theatrical conventions.

The play begins with the actors addressing the audience and explaining that certain lighting and musical effects will be created within the performing area. This serves to allay the children's potential fears of darkness and the occasional lighting blackout as well as preparing them for the sudden and at times strange synthesised sounds provided by the musicians.

Most importantly it invites children to seek out and identify those theatrical elements within the context of the performance. This technique serves to demystify the theatricality of the performance without detracting from the enjoyment of the story. It treats children as an intelligent audience capable of distinguishing between reality and fantasy; able to understand the concept of an actor in 'role', and able to appreciate that such elements as music, lighting, costumes and design are integral to the performance.

Music is an important component in all REM's work, particularly in *More Myths and Muses*. Many of the instruments used in REM's performances are extracted from the regions of the original myths. These include pan pipes, ockerina, flute, woodimba, thunder sheets and clapping sticks. A leitmotif accompanies the entrances of the characters during the performance and becomes a symbol of identification of the characters for the audience.

Wayan's instrument is the unusual ockerina, a small bowl shaped clay instrument, which produces soft melodic tones when blown into. This sound is the perfect accompaniment for the graceful, mystic movements that actress Annerose De Jong creates for the character of *Wayan*. The movements of *Wati-Kutjara*, the Lizard Man, played by Roger Rynd, are echoed by the rhythms and tones of the didgeridoo and the spritely, gibbering, *Velee* are accompanied by bamboo sticks.

Peter Winkler, composer and musician with REM theatre, is not only an important and integral member of the production team, with a wealth of experience as a teacher and composer, but was invaluable on the trip to Fiji. In an exchange of theatrical and production techniques at the University of the South Pacific, Peter demonstrated the musical instrument, the mouth harp. Students joined Peter in an improvised music session with their own version of a mouth harp made from coconut leaves.

At another time, the company were travelling on a boat to a nearby island. On the ferry were a group of school children who were singing and clapping. The natural rhythms and melodies of the songs were so energetic and hypnotic that Winkler brought out the tape recorders and recorded their singing. He incorporated these sounds and rhythms throughout *More Myths and Muses*. Evaluation notes from teachers and parents constantly referred to the music as an outstanding feature of the production, a feature that children also commented on long after the performance.

Clapping effects are used throughout the production — a voice for thunder; an accompaniment for running or a signal for detecting impending danger. Roger Rynd (1993) recalls an incidence which added impact to the importance of this sound effect,

We had used thunder in *Myths and Muses* by stomping our feet slowly and rhythmically on the ground. During one of the performances, a dancer from one of the villages ran up ecstatically saying that they also represent thunder by stomping their feet in the same rhythmic pattern.

R. Rynd, personal communication, March 2nd, 1993

Time and time again, the company was presented not only with the diversity of myth and storytelling of the Fijian culture, but also the surprising similarities in the reproduction of these myths in a performance context.

The set and costumes also reflect the company's travels. Found objects such as plaited rope, sacks, bamboo and fallen debris were used to replicate the surroundings that the company were exposed to in Fiji. Household mops became wigs for the mischievous *Velee*. A long, fibrous river root packed neatly away in a suitcase was woven into intricate foot and wrist bracelets. Fijian artefacts litter the stage performing area. Rituals are hinted at by the performers — "I'm just going to light the oil lamp now and then we can begin".

What is interesting about this process is Rem's fundamental desire to offer early childhood audiences an intelligent theatrical experience, that deconstructs the theatrical process while simultaneously using that process to introduce young audiences to the significance of myths and storytelling.

A question that might be raised is the appropriateness of this production for an early childhood audience. Are we expecting too much of this age group in their ability to grasp theatrical concepts? By inviting children not only to witness the drama but also identify and appreciate the theatricality of the performance, will their overall enjoyment of the story and spectacle be compromised?

The following comments made by children who attended performances of *More Myths and Muses* at Sydney's Opera House, in part, answer some of these questions.

I liked the velee cause they were funny, they always did things back to front and they could lift an elephant but not a feather and they had a mop for hair and I thought they played the music really really well and I liked the song they made up.

Sarah, aged 8.

I liked Pele the best because of her voice and her mask.

Toby, aged 7.

The best characters was the velee. They were excellent how they said everything backwards. I really liked the hair with the mops and feather on top. I thought you set it out really well. All the characters were excellent. I thought that the instrument man was excellent. He was very clever I think. It was great.

Samantha, aged 8.

I thought the lizard man was very funny the way he spoke. The lizard man was a very good actor. His real name was Roger.

Chloe, aged 7.

It is interesting to note the diversity of the comments. These children not only express their enjoyment of the play and the characters but can also specifically pinpoint the theatrical elements that contributed to their appreciation of the performance such as masks, costumes, and music.

Where once we might have expected comments such as, "I liked the big, bad wolf" or "My favourite character was Cinderella. She had a beautiful dress", it is interesting to note the comparative sophistication of the above responses. The process of demystifying the theatrical experience by REM theatre has not, I believe, detracted in any way from the pleasure gained by witnessing the play. Without external input, the child audience has deconstructed the performance by identifying theatrical concepts and elements such as costumes, music, masks and character movements and actions.

DE JONG, as 'PELE' the fire worman

REM Theatre
"Myths and Muses"

Of particular interest, is the response of Sarah, who mentions the *Velee* who can "lift an elephant but not a feather". Here she is acknowledging the comic characteristics of the *Velee* but is also identifying the costume of the velee — " the mops and feather on top'. This demonstrates an understanding of the complexity of character reflected in the text, the action and the costume. Also clearly understood, is the concept of an actor being in 'role' as evidenced by the child referring to the character, "the lizard man" and then, the actor, Roger, by name.

There is no reason why the production qualities of good children's theatre should not be as appealing to adults as to children. In this case, comments from parents and teachers indicate that this performance had such qualities.

The children were enthralled. I sat and watched 100 three year olds not stir for 45 minutes, they were so engrossed. . . . As president of the school committee I have a lot of contact with parents, and (they) were as enthralled as the kids.

Susan Christian, Chatswood, NSW

It is fabulous that someone is providing serious and real theatre for children. I think the children appreciate being respected as thinking human beings.

Tracey Gibson, Glebe, NSW

Children spent most of the two-hour train trip home discussing the use of costumes, music and sound effects. Many were anxious to try out the different movements of the characters. The teachers were just as enthusiastic about the performance as the children.

Kim King, Umina, NSW

Cross-cultural performances require sensitive handling. REM theatre has successfully reproduced Fijian myths through the traditional art of storytelling, coupled with the modern techniques of theatrical production. The company has paid particular attention to conveying the milieu and context of the myth in its original form. Fijian artefacts, musical instruments, rhythms, melodies, costumes and props that reflect the cultural context of the region, are all incorporated into the production.

We acknowledge that through dramatic play, children are acute observers of their world and are able to recreate, sometimes with meticulous details, scenes and events from their world, that incorporate multiple and complex characters, multifarious emotions and diverse and rigorous relationships. It is this fundamental understanding of children and children's play that is the centrepiece of REM's work. REM uses a play approach to create theatre and acknowledges that children are a discerning audience who can appreciate complexity of performance, narrative, character and theatrical effects. Such an audience deserves high quality, thought-provoking theatre.

---

[1] In an Artistic Report presented to the Australia Council at the conclusion of the project, REM state, ". . . our methods of performance (dance, music, narrative, and integration of the local language), has inspired the beginning of a Fijian contemporary theatre, integrating traditional myths and modes of performance with contemporary tales and technology. The development of this nascent theatre will be exciting to watch and hopefully, work with in '94."

[2] The General Manager of the Sydney Opera House, Mr Lloyd Martin, recently announced a sister relationship between the Sydney Opera House and a new centre for Performing Arts in Seoul, Korea. As part of the proposed cultural exchange, REM Theatre will be presenting a new version of *Myths and Muses* in Korea in 1993.

The arts curriculum and indigenous art: hands off or on? — A personal view

CHRISTINE STEVENSON

Institute of Early Childhood, Macquarie University

1993, declared the International Year of Indigenous People by UNICEF, is an appropriate time to look at the ways in which the arts of indigenous people are mediated in the curriculum. In this article I attempt to present some dilemmas faced by educators in confronting this issue and offer a personal perspective as a teacher educator in Australia. As an Australian, my experience has been more directly linked with Aboriginal culture, though I believe the issues are pertinent to most indigenous cultures.

In recent years, criticism of programs involving indigenous arts has been severe, leaving many educators with the feeling that "they're damned if they do and damned if they don't" become involved in such programs. The charge of ethnocentrism in relation to such programs is examined and found to have considerable substance. Activities selected from some Australian and North American programs are presented to highlight the problems involved. Other programs which show a sensitivity to the integrity of a culture and an awareness of children's needs are also discussed.

In an attempt to provide a more balanced viewpoint I have included several other perspectives on this issue: that of Ms Bronwyn Bancroft, renowned Aboriginal artist and those of two Aboriginal educators from the Aboriginal Early Childhood Services Support group within the Aboriginal Education Consultative Group, NSW Australia. Ms Bancroft chose to comment directly on the article (see footnotes). The views of Ms Jo Pender and Mr Ross Hughes appear in the Appendix 1.

Key words: Arts curriculum, indigenous art, ethnocentrism, early childhood

During a recent visit to an inner city pre-school in Sydney, I heard a voice "Hey everyone, Darryl's uncle is here with his didgeridoo." Children, teachers, and assistants moved spontaneously to the courtyard and listened eagerly to the music, moving their bodies in rhythmic response. This was not an activity pre-programmed for Aboriginal week so that teachers could satisfy requirements for "an Aboriginal perspective". Instead, it was an occasion that children had anticipated through word-of-mouth communication based on the reputation of Darryl's uncle. The spontaneity of the performance added to the sense of "naturalness", the feeling that the playing of the didgeridoo was an integral part of the everyday world of these children, who, when the music stopped, drifted back to the activities they had been engaged in.

ETHNOCENTRISM AND INDIGENOUS ART

Children now have the opportunity to see diverse new forms of Aboriginal art as the culture adapts to outside influences and Aboriginal artists increasingly undertake courses in art schools. Contemporary Aboriginal artwork incorporates many different media and techniques — clay, batik, printmaking and the ubiquitous acrylic on canvas. It has become fashionable to admire Aboriginal art and the market has responded in a fairly predictable way — the proliferation of Aboriginal designer T-shirts for purchase and the frequency of exhibitions of Aboriginal art in Australia, Europe and the U.S.A. are instances of the so-called "Renaissance" of Aboriginal art.[1]

As a visual arts educator in Australia, I have had mixed feelings in response to the intense interest shown in Aboriginal art over the past decade by teachers and the general community. On the one hand, I am excited by the potentially rich educational experiences which could result from such interest. The accessibility of Aboriginal artworks through frequent exhibitions in art galleries and through printed material such as books and posters should be welcomed by all educators. The change that has taken place since my childhood (where examples of Aboriginal art were placed in the context of so-called "primitive"[2] people who used "primitive" methods of decoration) is quite remarkable.

On the other hand, the kind of activities offered in educational settings in response to Aboriginal art raises concerns about cultural insensitivity and ethnocentrism. Despite the inundation of Aboriginal arts within the Australian public arena — and that includes popular music and dance as well as the visual arts — there is still a marked lack of knowledge about Aboriginal culture, in the Australian community and amongst educators.[3] This is reflected in the lack of respect shown for the culture in activities which are introduced to children to satisfy an "Aboriginal perspective" as for instance, taking part in a "corroboree", which is a sacred ceremony in Aboriginal communities, not merely a social occasion. Some students who are studying art as a General Studies subject in a teacher education program have quite innocently copied designs from Aboriginal artworks and incorporated them into their own work, not as any kind of postmodern comment, but in a way which seems to parallel the first white colonists' taking of the land belonging to the Aborigines over two hundred years ago. This attitude is also evident in the commercial world, where flagrant copy-

---

[1]Though Aboriginal art has achieved a profile in the world most of the entrepreneurs have been non-Aboriginal, and the monetary compensation for Aboriginal people and their communities has been minimal in comparison to the profits made by white entrepreneurs.

[2]It is incredible that a word like "primitive" could have been used to describe highly civilised religious ceremonies using secret, sacred images. This way of describing Aboriginal people is reflected in the law of white Australia which did not give Aboriginal people citizenship until 1967. It is also reflected in the time it has taken for Aboriginal Studies to become part of the school curriculum in Australia.

[3]Generally, I feel we, as a society, expect too much from Aboriginal people in terms of dissemination of information about themselves.

ing and trivialising of Aboriginal art is apparent on T-shirts, pamphlets and souvenirs.[4]

Some critics claim that this ethnocentric approach is impossible to avoid, no matter how sensitive teachers are. Anne Marie Willis, for example, a keynote speaker at the NSW Art Education Society Conference (May 1990), attempted to demonstrate how Aboriginal culture has been "repackaged" to suit the demands of "modernism" and how it has been compelled to "speak the words of the dominant culture". In an international art journal, she illustrates this point:

... the most obvious point of entry into the abstract forms of Aboriginal art is modernism. Thus the Western desert dot paintings (from the settlements such as Papunya, Yuendumu and Yuelumu), in which a complex and unknowable symbology of body painting and ground diagrams is transferred to canvas, often get read as abstract art. (Willis 1989a: 110):

This tendency to view cultures in terms of one's own, effectively confirms the superiority of Western society. Western society's translations of the Aboriginal "Dreaming" are collapsed into "legend, mythology, ancestors, gods or spirits." (Willis and Fry, 1989a: 110). For non-Aboriginals, Willis & Fry, (1989a) claim the spirituality that is often referred to, can never be accessed because they do not share the same system of beliefs and values.[4]

Willis (1990:12) presents the case clearly as follows:

Art is an ethnocentric category that Western culture has imposed on the material objects of non-Western cultures. It has removed objects from their traditions, where they may have functioned as practical artefacts or as items of ritual, and placed them in its museums for aesthetic contemplation. In fact art history has invented a special category to homogenise cultural difference — the category of primitive art. It is important to realise that 'primitive' is a label that the cultures so named would not apply to themselves.[5]

Fry and Willis (1989b: 5) have been critical of programs conducted by non-Aboriginal people, directed primarily at non-Aboriginal audiences claiming that these programs are counter-productive because they use an "intermediate class of mediators", that is white teachers, who continue to reproduce conditions of inequality. Refusal to become involved in these programs — a "hands off" approach — is thus seen as an affirmative act for critics like Willis and Fry. They claim that the only legitimate strategies are those which address issues of "cultural categorisations and ethnocentrism".

(Willis and Fry, 1989b: 6)[6].

---

[4]An advisory Board, Aboriginal Arts Management Association (A.A.M.A.) has been set up specifically to advise legislation needs to be introduced, such as a trademark for the authenticity of Aboriginal art and objects.
[5]This invites the question: Why have museums? Seriously, who asked the permission of Aboriginal communities to remove their sacred objects to an alien environment?
[6]I have a problem with these words. It seems that the issues can be debated without the consultation of Aboriginal people. This reinforces the idea that we can't talk about our own history and culture.

THE ROLE OF NON-INDIGENOUS EDUCATORS

Though the above argument sounds convincing and presents some strong evidence for exercising great care when presenting aspects of Aboriginal culture, I feel it would be welcomed by teachers who are uncomfortable with the inclusion of an Aboriginal perspective in programming and who would happily use the argument as an excuse to abandon an Aboriginal perspective. As Snow (1992: 4) has revealed in relation to teaching indigenous studies in New Zealand, "it was extremely tempting for me to leave Maori education aside". Snow's (1992: 5) conclusion is that "to leave the entire indigenous programme to Maori educators would be to leave the entire burden of decolonisation to them." In even blunter terms Snow (1992: 5) states "I saw that non-indigenous people had made the mess, and to leave it to indigenous people to clean up alone was a convenient and safe cop-out on my part."[7]

Arguments like those used by Fry and Willis (1989) are useful in highlighting the dangers involved in using art from another culture to find out more about that other culture (particularly when one of the cultures is in a more dominant position in society). We should be conscious of the following points in particular:

- that what is presented is altered by the authority of the presenter, who brings his/her own cultural perspective to the work/s.
- that Aboriginal culture is multi-faceted; there are many different cultural groups and no single representative voice for Aboriginal culture.[8] (This has implications for teachers who wish to seek approval for including specific activities in their program).
- that art cannot be separated from society.[9] (In traditional Aboriginal societies in particular the arts are integrated more fully with other aspects of life than they are in contemporary Western society).

Derman-Sparks (1989: 7) also warns early childhood teachers of the dangers of a "tourist curriculum" which teaches children about cultures through "artefacts of the culture" and fails to communicate real understanding of the culture. So, artworks that are treated as isolated objects lose contextual meaning or take on meanings from their new context which may convey insensitive or erroneous information.[10]

---

[7] I endorse this statement. We *all* have to strive to create a better environment and conditions for indigenous people.
[8] There *is* a very large voice for Aboriginal people, i.e. themselves. In non-Aboriginal society being diverse is acclaimed while in Aboriginal society it is sometimes interpreted as an indication of a lack of solidarity. The Aboriginal Educational Consultative Group (A.E.C.G.) does provide a "voice" for Aboriginal people.
[9] This is the lynch pin for the success of teaching Aboriginal programs. Aboriginal culture and life cannot be separated: it is all embracing.
[10] All art, I think, is evaluated on a number of criteria: visual impact, meaning and historical relevance.

For many years I had adopted a "hands off" approach to Aboriginal culture. My main defence was my lack of knowledge of Aboriginal culture and my belief that Aboriginal culture should be introduced by people from that culture. In the best of all possible worlds I would still hold with this attitude. The tendency to view other cultures through the cultural binoculars of one's own culture is difficult if not impossible to avoid. In spite of these misgivings I decided to question the "hands off" approach.[11]

The students who I currently teach are in engaged in preservice education to become teachers of young children. In NSW schools and in most other Australian states, it is mandatory to include an Aboriginal perspective in curriculum studies. The fact that most of these students will teach in centres and schools with no Aboriginal children does not permit the omission of an Aboriginal perspective. An Aboriginal perspective is important not just because Australia is culturally diverse, but because racism is still entrenched in Australian society in spite of the marked change in government attitudes, policies and programmes since the 1970's. However, at the tertiary level of education, apart from those who choose an Aboriginal Studies elective, many students will be graduating with a superficial knowledge of Aboriginal culture. Lack of understanding of Aboriginal culture results in inappropriate responses by students at the tertiary level.

The problem of my not being from an Aboriginal culture cannot be overlooked, but, in my opinion, should not lead to inaction on my part as a professional educator. As more Aboriginal students take up teaching positions in universities, my position in relation to teaching in the area of Aboriginal art and culture must obviously change.

In a recent article by Jones and Derman-Sparks (1992), I was reminded of some of the changes in attitude I was forced to undergo in taking on board the challenge of including an Aboriginal perspective in my Visual Arts course at the Institute of Early Childhood. Derman & Sparks (1992: 14) are at pains to remind us that "disequilibrium is never comfortable" but "it's a necessary condition for constructing new ways of thinking and doing." They suggest ways of facing up to potential obstacles which are in fact, similar to the strategies I used several years ago.

Derman & Sparkes' (1992: 15) suggestion is to "buddy up with a sympathetic colleague or two in your school or community". In my institution an Aboriginal colleague, Tricia Elliott, invited me to visit remote rural communities in NSW and Central Australia which have a large percentage of Aboriginal people in their communities. This gave me the opportunity to discuss changes I wanted to make in the General Studies art curriculum (at the tertiary level) and obtain valuable feedback from Aboriginal people. Ms Elliott was also invited to talk to my students about appropriations of Aboriginal designs. She explained how certain people in

---

[11]Obviously, when we learn something, the area is fraught with hidden dilemmas . . . but, learning is a gift for all people.
[12]A series of historical, economic and spiritual blows have contributed to the meagre graduation figures for Aboriginal students at Australian universities.

a particular clan had "ownership" of a particular story and design which was passed to another member at death. This struggle to understand another culture and the problems of "borrowing" designs from another culture had been a source of anxiety for an 18 year-old Sydney student, Ilana Solomon.

She had addressed these issues in a visual diary and then expressed her concerns in the following (unpublished) poem:

> There is a koori in the suburb next to my white,
>   Middle class school,
> And I, an art student, try to imagine what her life
>   Must be like.
> With "artists licence" I play with the ancient symbols
>   Of her ancestors,
> While she, a mother, works at the mundane domestic chores
>   Of mine.
>
> Free in my culture, I struggle to understand hers
> while she fights within herself, trapped between
>   Two worlds.
> I struggle to justify my borrowing
>   Of the art, of the world
> we have stolen from her.
>
> She fights her past, ignores landright signs
> but hisses at white police.
>
> We meet in my dreams, both are women
>   Both feel a loss.
> We live in a grey world, surrounded by
> Symbols of the city, masculine
>   Metal, emotionless.
> We dream of a time, of corroboree
> And safety — a friendly circle.
>
> I reject my housework and weave the
> Dreams into my paintings and poems.
>   She, more trapped than me
> beats an ancient rhythm with her tongue
> While she methodically hangs our dreams
>   On a clothes line.

CONTEXTUAL ISSUES

Through my contacts with the Aboriginal community I was in a position to invite others to enrich the art program. Peter McKenzie, an Aboriginal curator, showed to the tertiary students, stages in the execution of a ground painting by artists from the Yuendumu Community in the Northern Territory.[13] Students were

---

[13]These paintings from the Yuendumu community were taken to Paris by Peter McKenzie who curated an exhibition there entitled "Magiciens de la Terre" in 1989.

interested in the way ground paintings (which were intended to be temporary objects and part of a ceremony) have to a large extent been replaced by acrylic painting on canvas, a much more permanent artform. A discussion ensued as to how this evolution occurred. Critical issues were raised about the effect of the dominant culture's notions of art and the influence of modern publicity and commodity production on Aboriginal painting.

Thus, through the study of an aspect of Aboriginal art, important contextual issues arose and were debated. As Mechling (1990: 153) has observed, learning about other cultures should take place through "active pedagogy" and students must learn the skills of dialogue. Mechling, (1990: 53) also reminds us that "analysing a particular cultural 'text' can lead to other texts and to ever widening patterns of meaning". The "text" in my example was the process involved in the making of the ground painting. The "texts" included acrylic paintings and other forms of Aboriginal art and their wider meanings. It has to be said that some students found this dialogue confronting and became quite hostile at the implications of ethnocentrism involved in the discussion on Aboriginal art as commodity production. But as Mechling (1990: 160) is at pains to point out:

... teachers and students alike must learn to become comfortable with anxiety, uncertainty, and even fear. Too often, instructors avoid risk-taking behaviour, more often censoring themselves than facing the imagined consequences of experimenting and failing. Undoubtedly, teachers and students will experience unfamiliar and unsettling moments in the multicultural dialogue.... Students and faculty members will encounter levels of anger that do not usually surface in the traditional classroom.

THE ARTS CURRICULUM

In arts curricula in Australian schools there is a strong emphasis on responding to mediated images. For instance, in the NSW Department of Education *Visual Arts Syllabus and Support Documents K-6* (1990: 25) it is stressed that:

Students need to discover meaning for themselves in mediated images and this can be encouraged by ... having them create artworks from mediated images.

This can be a dangerous strategy and can lead to mis-appropriation of designs *if the first part of the statement is ignored.* Some activities I have observed in schools fall into this category. For example, seven year old children in an urban Australian setting were invited to decorate a boomerang with traditional designs and to use emus, snakes and wild dingoes as subject matter. We need to examine what kind of meanings are being transmitted in such an experience and to be mindful of the sacredness of some symbols in Aboriginal culture.

Similar concerns are expressed by educators in the USA. Jane Billman (1992: 22) points out that:

Preschool teachers don't teach the essence of what is Native American because we don't know the Native American culture.... Typically, preschool, kindergarten, and primary curricula include the standard activities of making Indian headbands, totem poles, and tepees.

She goes on to explain:

Totem poles and tepees are products of the lifestyles of only a few tribes of Indians.... Headdresses were not simply for decoration — feathers in headbands were symbols of achievements or acts of bravery. (Billman 1992: 22).

At the tertiary level, it may be possible to initiate dialogue about cultural attitudes to the land, from a non-Aboriginal and from an Aboriginal perspective.[14] For example, reverence for the land and the ancestral past of Aborigines is shown in the following anecdote of Galarrwuy Unupingu, son of Arnhem Land artist Munggurrawuy (cited by Sutton, 1988: 13-14):

When I was 16 years old my father taught me to sing some of the songs that talk about the land.... One day, I went fishing with Dad. As I was walking along behind him I was dragging my spear on the beach which was leaving a long line behind me. He told me to stop doing that. He continued telling me that if I made a mark, or dig, with no reason at all, I've been hurting the bones of the traditional people of the land. We must only dig and make marks on the ground when we perform or gather food.

SENSITIVE PROGRAMMING

Is it possible to transmit this reverence for the land to children? In relation to indigenous Americanism, Polly Greenberg points out (1992: 80):

We are probably teaching children a more authentic understanding of an aspect of traditional Native Americanism when we do any of the following than when we help children glue construction paper feathers onto their tagboard headbands: feel the sun burning fiercely off our skin and the sand; watch with awe a flaming orange sunset set over cliff-like red rocks; explore forests and quarries, gurgling brooks, and dry creekbeds; walk around a swampy sweet gum woods; smell sandhill pines or salty seaweed — scented ocean breezes; see spiders weaving dew-silvered webs in early morning sunlight; observe butterflies — pure silk and flutter; ...

Art director, Ursula Kolbe, at the Child and Family Study Centre, Institute of Early Childhood, Macquarie University, plans to introduce an Aboriginal perspective to preschoolers by collecting sands of various hues and textures, observing that "a consciousness of sand appears to be an integral part of Aboriginal culture, centering as it does on a deep relationship with the land." In

---

[14] For any dialogue about cultural attitudes to the land to be fruitful, we must first put equal status on the two perspectives: Aboriginal and non-Aboriginal.

Figure 1 Six year old child's drawing of the area surrounding her school *before* teacher had introduced children to examples of Aboriginal art.

this way children can be introduced to Aboriginal thinking about the land in a more child-centred way. (See Appendix 2 for a fuller description of the planned program).

Wendy Atkins, a teacher of six-year-olds at an inner city Sydney school, uses a different approach. She encourages children to use their own symbols to make a map of their playground *before* introducing an Aboriginal painting which shows another way of representing that person's relationship to their land. [See Fig. 1] After children have been introduced to other examples of Aboriginal painting, she asks the children to "tell" their own stories about their lives using symbols. [See Figs. 2-4].

Dianne Snow (1992), a tertiary educator, used another approach after pondering the question:

How could I actually teach Aboriginal studies as a non-Aboriginal person, while not setting myself up as authoritative about Aboriginality and Aboriginal knowledge[16]

Some of the strategies Snow, (1992) found useful include:

- telling the class I was not Aboriginal, which meant I could not speak from a position of authority;

---

[16]Authoritative notions can be dangerous in teaching. The skill is to impart fair and accurate information.

Figure 2

Figure 3

- inviting as many Aboriginal speakers as possible to talk to the class, who would be speaking from a position of authority;
- always drawing on Aboriginal authors (or prior speakers) during classroom discussion, rather than presenting my own opinion, and;

Figure 4

Figures 2-4 Responses to selected Aboriginal artworks by six-year old children at Annandale North Public School. Teacher: Ms Wendy Atkins.

- indicating when I was giving my own "best guess" in response to questions where neither I nor the students could draw on Aboriginal authors/speakers.

It is important for non-aboriginal educators to collaborate with Aboriginal colleagues wherever possible. For instance, Tricia Elliot, my Aboriginal colleague collaborated with me in presenting a workshop for early childhood personnel entitled *Using Aboriginal artworks as a stimulus for artmaking with young children* (at various venues throughout New South Wales). One of the activities we offered involved an analysis of learning experiences devised by students at the Institute of Early Childhood, Macquarie University. The plans were critiqued from both an Aboriginal perspective and from a creative arts perspective. In this way, we were able to usefully draw upon the expertise of each presenter. The workshop gave us an opportunity to *begin* to challenge some practices which we perceived as negative in early childhood settings and to begin to discuss practices which we saw as more appropriate. Some of the issues/questions discussed included:

- the problem of reinforcing stereotypes of Aboriginal people (in particular that Aboriginal people are *only* good at art).
- the problem of introducing an Aboriginal perspective with limited media such as earth colours and encouraging the children to paint with dots on bark (thus reinforcing the notion of Aboriginal art as resistant to change).
- the need to use resources which reflect the richness and diversity of contemporary Aboriginal society such as twined dilly bags, carved wooden implements, acrylic paintings, linoprints — (difficult when resources in schools and early childhood settings are often limited).

- the need to show how symbols are owned by various groups of Aboriginal people and should not be borrowed without permission. (This discourages the tendency particularly observed in schools of encouraging children to copy patterns they discover in Aboriginal artworks). Another problem associated with the "translation" of symbols is the potential practice of reducing Aboriginal art to an easily read system of signs. (See Appendix 3). A fear was expressed that Aboriginal art could be perceived as completely accessible as long as we know the meaning of the symbols. Since there is no uniform set of symbols in Aboriginal art and some are kept secret within the group, care needs to be exercised. Even more worrying was the view that this approach could lead to a perception of Aboriginal art as a kind of map-making. (See Footnote 15).

In summary, the following words of Aboriginal poet, Daisy Utemorrah (1990: 3) could be used to highlight the dilemmas involved in the issue of including indigenous arts in the curriculum.

> Do not go around the edges
> or else you'll fall.
> No good that place
> or else you slip.

Is this a warning to stay out of territory that we don't fully understand or is it an exhortation to stop being fence-sitters ...? The challenge of enriching the curriculum with programmes sensitive to the integrity of the indigenous arts cannot be ignored. Educators need to work collaboratively to create programmes which not only reflect the cultural dynamics of their communities but which also develop stronger relationships between indigenous and non-indigenous peoples.

Appendix 1: Responses to the issue by two Early Childhood educators

The notion of being in a state of paralysis over the inclusion of Aboriginal culture into the program is an issue for many people and education services. It is coincidentally an issue for Aboriginal as well as non-Aboriginal people.

I consider that it is better to "stick out one's neck" as an educator rather than remain in the state of paralysis. It is better to include some activity or technique and infringe the sensibilities of some person than to not deal with Aboriginal culture. However, this action must not be seen as a position which should not be retreated from. A suggestion from an Aboriginal person about the unsuitability of the activity would mean its withdrawal and seeking the opinion of that person for a suitable alternative. It is too important an issue to deal with the original Australian culture. Aboriginal people do not necessarily have detailed information

---

[15] This is problematic: this could be seen as a way of "map-making" and may limit the levels of meaning and the dynamic impact of the work.

on sacredness of cultural information or techniques and their suitability for inclusion in educational curriculum. This is only to be expected with non-Aboriginal oppression of the last 205 years. In addition, the history of the period of oppression is a period which has been expressed in Aboriginal culture throughout the period and in contemporary times.

Certainly, the process of consultation is very important but the absence of people or consultative processes should not mean that no action can take place.

Ross Hughes
Aboriginal educator,
Aboriginal Early Childhood Support Unit (A.E.C.G.)
NSW, Australia.

I believe there should be a "hands-on" approach to Aboriginal Studies. I feel that for too long there has been a "hands-off" approach and this is one of the main contributors to the ignorance and racist attitudes towards Aboriginal people in general.

The last few years have looked a lot more positive as Aboriginal art has become more popular along with music and dance. However, the art of our people still needs protection since the exploitation of Aboriginal art is ever threatening.

When teaching art at any level it is important to be informed. People need to be sensitive to community needs. My advice is to seek an Aboriginal artist to come into the centre and paint or perform for you.

In areas where you are unable to find any community information/support, it is still important to uncover the history and find out about the art, methods, materials, etc. Rather than having students copy art, encourage them to use the techniques to see what it was like to paint traditionally.

A "hands-on" approach can only open doors of understanding to the wider society. It is important to be culturally sensitive and to use local communities, where possible.

Jo Pender
Aboriginal educator,
Aboriginal Early Childhood Support Unit (A.E.C.G.)
NSW, Australia.

Appendix 2: Aboriginal Perspective in the Early Childhood Curriculum

Background

Aboriginal art is frequently introduced in primary schools through activities which encourage children to imitate or adopt certain Aboriginal artistic "styles" (eg. dot paintings), and use traditional "Aboriginal" colours (earth tones, red, yellow & black) and implements such as sticks for painting. Such imposition of artistic practices is not seen as appropriate in early childhood education. If artistic methods and processes are to have meaning for the child (indeed, any artist), these should in the first instance, emanate from the child's own cognitive and emotional needs interwoven with the child's manipulation of, and interaction with, media.

Plan

As a starting point, at the Child and Family Study Centre, we propose to seek commonalities between the children's interests and such elements in Aboriginal culture to which young children can easily relate. Accordingly, our focus will begin with sand play. A consciousness of sand appears to be an integral part of Aboriginal culture, centering as it does on a deep relationship with the land. Sand has been traditionally used in Aboriginal culture as a medium for storytelling and even today, has been observed to be used by some as a medium for making preparatory sketches and designs (rather than on paper) for contemporary acrylic paintings.

We will begin by collecting sands of various hues and textures. The sand will be introduced on trays for children's spontaneous exploration and drawing. Gradually we will use the sand trays as a talking point for aspects of the Aboriginal people and culture — to be expanded through stories and picture books, and looking at artefacts. (Over time, we plan to involve children in collecting and displaying glass jars filled with sands.)

Ursula Kolbe
*Lecturer in Visual Arts,
Art Director, Child & Family Study Centre,
Institute of Early Childhood, Macquarie University*

Appendix 3: Aboriginal Symbols and Meanings

(Hall 1992: 52)

Dots:	Have a meaning of water, rain, people, places and tracks
Cross Hatching:	Lines running into each other have a meaning of measuring distances and representing the land
Wave Lines:	These lines can represent many different things such as the ocean, rivers, mountains, tracks, snakes and also distances
Spirals:	Representing a water sign, it has many meanings depending on the artist, such as Billabongs, Waterholes, Springs and the Rainbow Serpent
Plain Circles:	These can be waterholes, Special Places, Dancing Grounds. A Whole Tribal Area etc.
Circles Within Circles:	Camp Sites, Places of Special Importance.
Camp Fire:	Two lines crossed within a circle.

These are some examples of Aboriginal art symbols. There are many more and these symbols were used throughout Australia by some Aboriginal people.

References

Billman, J. (1992) The Native American curriculum: attempting alternatives to tepees and headbands. *Young Children*. September; 22-25

Derman-Sparks, L. and the A.B.C. Task Force (1989) *Anti-bias curriculum: tools for empowering young children*. Washington D.C.: National Association for the Education of Young Children

Greenberg, P. (1992) Teaching about Native Americans? Or teaching about people, including Native Americans? Young Children. September: 27-30, 79-80

Hall, L. (1992) Visual arts education K-6: an Aboriginal perspective. *Journal of Aboriginal Studies Association*. 2: 27-62

Jones, E. and Derman-Sparks, L. (1992) Meeting the challenge of diversity. *Young children* Jan 1992; 12-16

Mechling, J. (1990) Theory and the other; or, is this session the text? *American Behavioural Scientist*, 34: 153-164

New South Wales Department of Education (1989). *Visual arts K-6 syllabus and support documents*. Sydney: NSW Department of Education

Snow, D. (1992) Teaching indigenous studies: some issues and strategies for non-indigenous teachers. (Paper presented to the Second Annual Aboriginal Studies Association Conference, University of New South Wales, Sydney, Australia. Sept. 28-30, 1992)

Willis, A. and Fry, T. (1989a) Aboriginal art: symptom or success. *Art in America*, July 1989: 110-118

Willis, A. & Fry, T. (1989b) Thinking in the shadows of neo-colonialism. Praxis M Vol 25, December 1989: 4-12

Willis, A. (1990) Ethnocentrism and culture. *Contemporary issues*, a collection of papers delivered at the Art Education Society of NSW Conference, Sydney Australia

Utemorrah, D. (1990) *Do not go around the edges*. Broome: Western Australia. Magabala Books

'Not wilting flowers again!' problem finding and problem solving in movement and performance

SUZANNE M. DYER and WENDY SCHILLER

School of Early Childhood Studies, Macquarie University, Australia

This paper outlines a process-oriented approach to teaching movement and performance that integrates the theoretical aspects of movement with a practical teaching method. The approach applies a play and problem solving model, which focuses on the creative process rather than creation of a product, to development of a method of teaching that encourages problem finding and problem solving. The teacher's role in this process is that of facilitator. Participants are encouraged to take responsibility for identifying a problem and solving that problem, and in the process, develop improved communication skills, interpersonal skills, and self confidence. Positive effects, as well as potentially limiting factors are discussed in terms of teaching the process to early childhood trainee teachers.

Key words: problem finding, problem solving, movement, performance, trainee teachers

INTRODUCTION

Recollections of end-of-year school performances reveal the terror of freezing on stage, forgetting what comes next, making grand entrances at the wrong time, turning one too many somersaults and falling off the stage, or being removed from the situation by a distraught teacher. Add to this the hours of repetitive practice that precede such *memorable* events, and the question needs to be asked, 'Why have school performances at all?' The answer to this is obvious — parents and relatives like to see their children perform, some children enjoy performing, and some teachers see it as an opportunity to highlight the year's work. Performance also affords an opportunity for assessment by, and accountability to, the community, and can be a showcase for school achievement. For these reasons, it would seem certain that the end-of-year performance is here to stay. But are these performances meaningful for children, and if not, then how can they be made meaningful?

Too often performance in early childhood centres and schools has minimal learning value for teachers and students, with repetition and rehearsal taking precedence over child-centred problem solving and decision making. This is not to say that performances should be discontinued. On the contrary, performance that is process-oriented, and based on the developmental needs, interests and ideas of the children can provide much enjoyment and valuable learning. This paper considers a process-oriented approach to performance as it relates to movement in the early childhood curriculum.

PROBLEM SOLVING AND PROBLEM FINDING

Theoretically, the preferred way of working in an early childhood movement class is to proceed from free play and exploration, through guided discovery to problem solving, with a direct instructional approach used only when refinement of skills or patterns is appropriate (Wetton, 1988; Gallahue, 1989). Problem solving, which is an integral part of the learning process (Sylva, 1984; Bruner, 1986), allows children to respond to a problem and identify one or many answers. That is, problem solving is open ended. Children can try the various solutions they have proposed to see which one best suits their purpose. This important strategy allows for individual approaches to learning, and encourages children to play creatively with ideas (Almy, Monighan, Scales & Van Hoorn, 1984; Klugman & Smilansky, 1990).

Problem solving has been extensively researched (Vandenberg, 1980), and is widely used within the early childhood movement curriculum (Wetton, 1988; Gallahue, 1989). However, little attention has been given to recognition of the process of *identifying* a problem, that is, 'problem finding' (Tegano, Sawyers & Moran, 1989). Children's play leads naturally to problem finding as play is spontaneous, and involves construction and reconstruction, experimentation, risking taking and testing. Furthermore, children who are encouraged to problem find "are more apt to learn generalizable skills and ... [are] better equipped to cope with real life problems than children who are presented with teacher-made problems and then taught one specific, 'right' solution" (Tegano et al., 1989. p. 97). Unfortunately, many teachers are so anxious to turn every encounter into an occasion for teaching or an opportunity to check on prior learning (Wells, 1986), that they do not consciously attend to this process, and therefore miss valuable opportunities to encourage children to develop problem finding skills.

A PLAY AND PROBLEM SOLVING MODEL APPLIED TO MOVEMENT AND PERFORMANCE

Tegano *et al.* (1989) have proposed a play and problem solving model which can be applied to movement in early childhood (Fig. 1). The model illustrates how outcomes vary according to the amount of time available, and whether a problem is discovered by the children themselves, or is presented to them by a teacher. In proposing this model, Tegano *et al.* (1989) have clearly illustrated that the teacher's role is a critical one. When the teacher is the facilitator and children

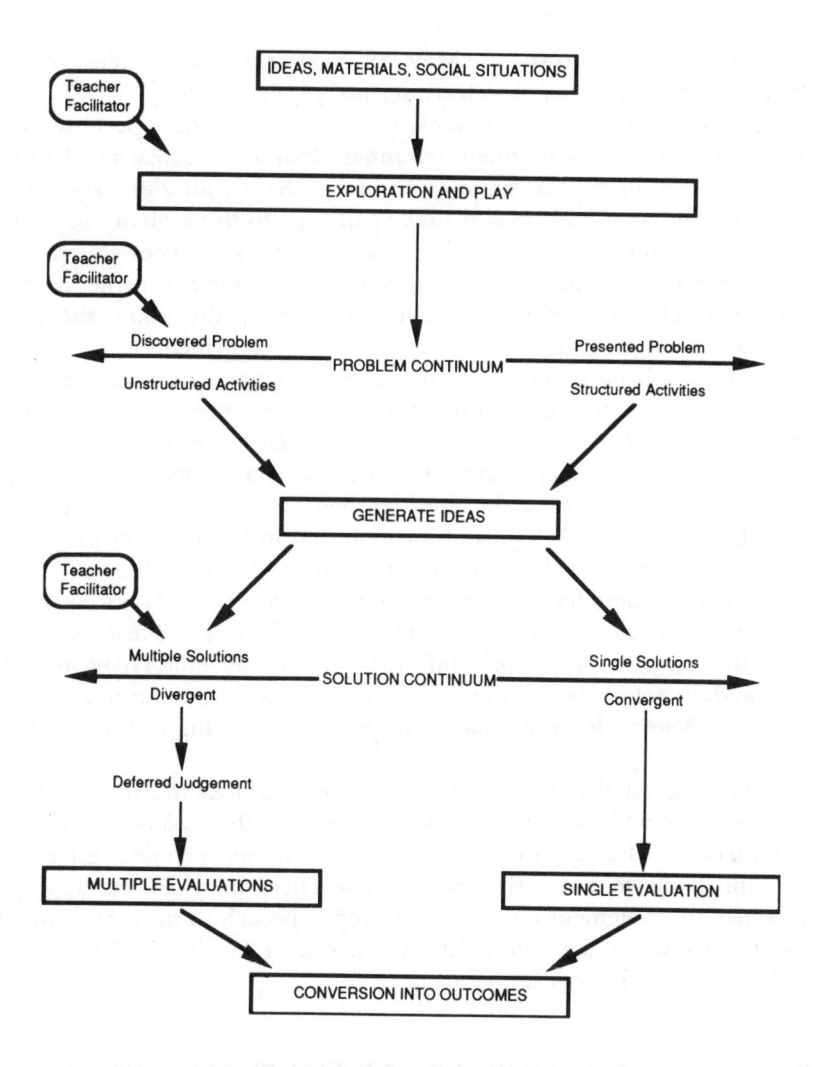

```
                    IDEAS, MATERIALS, SOCIAL SITUATIONS
  Teacher                        │
  Facilitator                    │
         ↘                       ↓
                    ┌─────────────────────────┐
                    │  EXPLORATION AND PLAY   │
                    └─────────────────────────┘
  Teacher                        │
  Facilitator                    │
         ↘                       ↓
  ← Discovered Problem    PROBLEM CONTINUUM    Presented Problem →
    Unstructured Activities                    Structured Activities
                    ↘         ↓         ↙
                    ┌─────────────────┐
                    │  GENERATE IDEAS │
                    └─────────────────┘
  Teacher              ↙                ↘
  Facilitator
         ↘
    ← Multiple Solutions   SOLUTION CONTINUUM   Single Solutions →
      Divergent                                 Convergent
           │                                         │
      Deferred Judgement                             │
           ↓                                         ↓
    ┌──────────────────────┐              ┌──────────────────┐
    │ MULTIPLE EVALUATIONS │              │ SINGLE EVALUATION│
    └──────────────────────┘              └──────────────────┘
                    ↘                ↙
                    ┌─────────────────────────┐
                    │ CONVERSION INTO OUTCOMES│
                    └─────────────────────────┘
```

Figure 1 Play and Problem Solving Model.

are the problem finders and solvers, multiple and divergent solutions will be proposed by the children; the process is more important than the product. The alternative, teacher-dominated approach, is time efficient, but relies heavily on teacher input, structured experiences, and presentation of a single problem which leads to a single solution; the product is more important than the process (Mosston & Ashworth, 1986). A teacher-dominated approach may not facilitate child-centred learning or allow sufficient time for children to construct, reconstruct, experiment with, and reflect upon, ideas. This is an important point in light of evidence suggesting that reconstruction of ideas, collaborative interaction and provision of a period of reflection are crucial to the development of children's intellectual growth (Bruner, 1983; Wells, 1986). As reflection and active reconstruction are also part of the creative process (May, 1975), a teacher-dominated approach can militate against creativity and learning for young children.

Unfortunately, the approach commonly used when developing performances in early childhood centres more often resembles that of the teacher-dominated approach. Instead of using performance as part of the learning process, whereby children are the decision makers and time is allowed to think about and develop an idea, teachers tend to take control and set specific sequences which may or may not be contextually appropriate. That is, the performance becomes a set piece devised by the teacher and rehearsed by the children. At this point, the learning process breaks down and the performance becomes contrived.

Two reasons have been suggested for this adult-dominated approach to teaching movement. First, prior to school entry, learning experiences for young children are at the discretion of parents, while movement experiences at school predomiantly focus on skill development, and are at the discretion of teachers (Halverson, 1988). As a result, attitudes and values learned have tended to be reinforced throughout life (Gallahue, 1989), and are reflected in the types of programmes implemented by trainee teachers and teachers alike (Schiller, 1991).

Second, many teachers have not been exposed to a process-oriented approach to movement, and thus, do not feel confident using it in an educational setting. Indications that teachers are poorly informed about why motor development is important, and do not recognize the types of activity and teaching strategies most appropriate for young children, may also contribute to this lack of confidence (Gallahue, 1989).

The authors suggest that by physically working through the process-oriented approach to movement, trainee teachers can overcome these constraints, and can begin to understand the meaning of problem finding and problem solving. The pre-service programme for early childhood teachers provides an appropriate forum in which to implement a process-oriented approach to movement and performance and focus on the role of the teacher as a facilitator. The following sections discuss such a programme.

A PROCESS-ORIENTED APPROACH TO MOVEMENT AND PERFORMANCE FOR TRAINEE TEACHERS

Before undertaking study related to teaching movement using a process-oriented approach, it is desirable for trainee teachers completing pre-service programmes in early childhood education to have knowledge of child development and curriculum planning, as well as experience with guided teaching practice in early childhood settings. This knowledge can then be used as a basis for a) experiencing, and making meaningful, problem finding and problem solving in a movement context, and b) developing teaching skills associated with facilitation of the process-oriented approach as outlined previously (Fig. 1).

In the programme discussed here, trainee teachers are initially introduced to the Laban framework (Copple, Sigel & Saunders, 1979), the phases of motor development as outlined by Gallahue (1989), appropriate teaching strategies for movement (Wetton, 1988; Gallahue, 1989), and a planning process which specifically draws on other areas of the curriculum, including drama, art, music and literature, in order to provide stimuli for movement experiences and exploration of concepts (Boorman, 1976; Stinson, 1988).

Trainee teachers then participate in a series of practical workshops which enables them to work at their own level (that is, as adults), and hence, to understand the process-oriented approach to movement and performance. Initial workshops provide a framework within which trainee teachers can comfortably take risks and experiment with multiple and divergent ways of approaching a problem. The lecturer's role at this point is not to provide answers to questions asked, but to be accessible, listen to concerns and, if necessary, assist with refocussing.

As trainee teachers become more aware of the process, and realize that there is no right or wrong way to proceed, the level of structure and input offered by the lecturer necessarily decreases. At this stage, trainee teachers need time to consolidate, reflect upon, and actively reconstruct their ideas. As well, it is important that they interact collaboratively, make connections with other curriculum areas, and reach consensus on ways of communicating their ideas through performance. Continued refinement and restructuring occurs until resolution is arrived at.

Final workshops typically involve performances which have evolved completely from trainee teacher input. That is, small groups of trainee teachers select suitable stimuli, experiment with ideas, identify a movement problem based on these stimuli and ideas, and work through possible solutions to create a piece of work which is then performed for, and critiqued by, peers.

PROFESSIONAL, PERSONAL AND CREATIVE DEVELOPMENT WITHIN THE PROCESS-ORIENTED APPROACH

Within the process-oriented approach to movement and performance, three areas of development which impinge on the teacher's role have been identified by the authors. These include creative, professional and personal development. As part of creative development, trainee teachers learn to translate two dimensional forms into three dimensional images, integrate and combine media and technology, and communicate aesthetic qualities through movement.

In terms of professional development, trainee teachers experience the steps involved in teaching movement using a process-oriented approach. These include identifying a movement problem which is suitable for exploration, recognizing the point at which the problem becomes an issue for further refinement and possible performance, and showing how they would develop the process as part of an overall curriculum plan.

Trainee teachers are also involved in a process of personal development. In the early part of the process, they learn to tolerate and cope with ambiguity in group discussions, be open and empathetic towards others, and experiment with ideas until a concept becomes clear, a theme evolves, and a sequence emerges.

Competence and confidence grows as trainee teachers develop a sense of ownership in relation to the problem they have created, and accept responsibility for changing the problem in order to refine or change direction, or even abandon a particular concept or course of action.

PROBLEMS IN THE PROCESS

Based on feedback from staff and trainee teachers involved in a movement programme using the process-oriented approach, a number of potentially limiting factors have been identified. These include difficulties associated with:

- exercising creative choice due to a lack of confidence and/or previous movement experience;
- recognizing the point at which ideas become translatable into something which could be communicated to an audience — this may also cause conflict within the group;
- conceptualizing an idea which may lead to performance — more often, teachers have a performance in mind (product) and work backwards to an idea that will fit the end product, which means that rote learning takes precedence over problem solving;
- accepting the fact that the end product is not the important component and is not initially known when the process commences;
- remaining open to possibilities which may arise, rather than imposing intentions, expectations or time limitations on the process;
- teacher trainees' feelings of vulnerability in being exposed to a process designed for use with children;
- teacher trainees' lack of trust that the individual components of the curriculum plan will come together to form a cohesive performance;
- accepting that some restructuring of a performance may be necessary as a result of showing work to other people and inviting comment;

It is the authors' firm belief that self confidence plays an important role in limiting the effects of factors listed above, both in terms of implementing the process, and participating in it. The programme discussed in this paper places a great deal of emphasis on providing an atmosphere that encourages decision making and accepts all solutions as being valid, as it is within this type of environment that confidence will increase (Schempp, 1983).

POSITIVE EFFECTS OF THE PROCESS

A process-oriented approach to movement and performance allows staff to team teach, thus providing trainee teachers with different perspectives and opinions, and a collaborative model of teaching which simulates the problem finding and problem solving approach inherent in the programme. Teachers learn to remain open to students' divergent ideas, to take risks, to have faith in the process, and to facilitate (rather than control) resolutions within the allowable time frame. That is, "the teacher accepts the notion that developing the ability of divergent, cognitive production is one of the goals of physical education" (Mosston & Ashworth, 1986, p. 196).

Trainee teachers participating in the programme identified as important, the "hands on" approach to movement, as well as the opportunity to put theory into practice. The practical nature and realistic approach to situations which trainee teachers are likely to encounter upon entrance to "the real world" of teaching was seen as being "inspirational, and showed how movement is achievable within fun contexts, ... [as well as being] a chance to explore our own creativity and imagination ... without losing sight of the whole focus on child-centredness, creativity and self esteem" (SETS, 1992).

Experience with the process of problem finding and problem solving in movement and performance also gave trainee teachers an understanding of the purpose of movement in relation to performance, and the confidence to use this process to teach movement. Furthermore, trainee teachers indicated that participation provided a chance to define the importance of movement, try out their own theory, and determine ways in which the process would work with children in early childhood settings (SETS, 1992). In the words of one trainee teacher, "it was a chance to let go and have a bit of fun, as well as inspiring me to structure a challenging and creative movement environment and programme for young children" (SETS, 1992).

CONCLUSION

The process-oriented approach to movement and performance discussed in this paper provides an avenue for the learner to become an independent and divergent thinker, and in the process, improves communication skills, interpersonal skills, and self confidence. Problem finding and problem solving help "develop greater independence in both cognition and physical responses, ... and actually demonstrate the cognitive-physical relationship in its various dimensions" (Mosston & Ashworth, 1986, p. 223). That is, they afford an opportunity to learn the relationship between cognitive production and physical performance. However, rather than being an end in itself, this process raises the issue posed by Kagan (1992) in relation to readiness — does learning precede development?

References

Almy, M., Monighan, P., Scales, B. and Van Hoorn, J. (1984) Recent research play: The teacher's perspective. In *Current Topics in Early Childhood Educaion Vol. 5.* edited by L.G. Katz. Norwood, N.J.: Ablex. pp. 1–25
Boorman, J. (1976) *Lesson Planning in Creative Dance in the First Three Grades.* London: Longman
Bruner, J. (1983) *Child's Talk.* London: Oxford University Press

Bruner, J. (1986) *Actual Minds, Possible Worlds.* Cambridge, MA: Harvard University Press

Copple, C., Sigel, I.E. and Saunders, R. (1979) *Educating the Young Thinker.* New York: Van Nostrant

Gallahue, D.A. (1989) *Understanding Motor Development: Infants, Children, Adolescents.* 2nd. ed. Indianapolis: Benchmark Press

Halverson, L.E. (1988) Motor development and physical education for young children. In *Moving and Learning for the Young Child* edited by W.J. Stinson. Presentations from the early childhood conference Forging linkages between moving and learning for preschool children. Washington DC, December 1-4, AAPHERD, pp. 85-103

Kagan, S.L. (1992) Readiness past, present and future: shaping the agenda. *Young Children.* **48**, 48-53

Klugman, E. and Smilansky, S. (Eds.). (1990) *Children's Play and Learning Perspectives and Policy Implications.* New York: Teacher's College Press

May, R. (1975) *The Courage to Create.* New York: Bantam Books

Mosston, M. and Ashworth, S. (1986) *Teaching Physical Education, 3rd. Ed.* Columbus: Merrill

Schempp. P.G. (1983) Influence of decision-making on attitudes, creativity, motor skills and self-concept in elementary children. *Research Quarterly,* **540**, 183-189

Schiller, W. (1991) Kindergyms for young children in the 80's: hothousing, hoax or happening?. *Early Child Development and Care.* **72**, 81-91.

SETS (Student Evaluation of Teaching and Subject), (1992) Macquarie University, Sydney, Australia

Stinson, S. (1988) *Dance for Young Children — Finding the Magic in Movement.* Reston, VA: AAHPERD

Sylva, K. (1984) A hard-headed look at the fruits of play. *Early Child Development and Care,* **15**, 171-184.

Tegano. D.W., Sawyers, J.K. and Moran, J.D. (1989) Problem-finding and solving in play. *Childhood Education,* winter, 192-197.

Vandenberg, B. (1980) Play, problem solving, and creativity. In *New Direction for Child Development: Children's Play* edited by K. Rubin. San Francisco: Jossey-Bass

Wells, G. (1986) *The Meaning Makers.* London: Heinemann

Wetton, P. (1988) *Physical education in the nursery and infant school.* London: Croom Helm

Introducing young children to live orchestral performance

LOUIE SUTHERS

Institute of Early Childhood, Macquarie University

Live performance provides an experience that cannot be matched by listening to recorded music in the classroom. The Sydney Symphony Orchestra has devised a program of concerts specifically for children in the first three years of school. The performances are designed to be developmentally appropriate for children aged from five to eight years. This paper outlines the innovate nature of the concerts that feature children as a participatory audience. The selection of repertoire and the types of support and resources provided for teachers are also discussed.

Key words: Music, Music education, Listening, Performance, Orchestra

Live performance adds a dimension to a program of musical listening that is not possible through recordings. To *see* the musicians play their instruments, to *hear* the sounds they make, to *watch* the conductor perform and *become aware of the interactions* between different players and *observe the patterns* in the music, is to really experience the orchestra.

"What's that"

A five-year old pointed towards the group of double basses at the side of the orchestra.

"A big, huge violin."

Sssssshhh.

"It's starting. . . . It's so big! So big!" The music from the orchestra filled the auditorium, wrapping the audience of excited, wide-eyed children in symphonic sounds. A big sound; a big group of musicians and a big experience for young children.

In 1990, the Sydney Symphony Orchestra (S.S.O.) introduced concerts specifically for children in Kindergarten (the first year of school) to Year 2; children aged from five to eight years. These K-2 concerts were innovate in many respects. This report reviews the program and outlines so ne of the features that have been important in its implementation.

SYDNEY SYMPHONY ORCHESTRA EDUCATION PROGRAM

The Sydney Symphony Orchestra has had a long tradition of concert-giving for young people. Since its formation in the 1930s, concerts for school children have been an important part of the orchestra's program. However, most of the schools concerts were designed for older primary and secondary students. Until recently.

Many changes from the standard fifty minute to hour-long schools' program held in the Concert Hall of the Sydney Opera House or Sydney Town Hall had to be made to meet the needs of such young concertgoers. An audience of silent six-year olds, listening attentively and politely applauding at the conclusion of each item did not seem an appropriate expectation for very young children. In consultation with teachers and other educators, Mary Vallentine , the S.S.O.'s general manager and the orchestra's education officer, Brett Johnson devised a new concert format. The K-2 programs needed to ". . . reach children on their own level with the highest quality music and the highest quality performance." (Johnson, 1990). Thus an informal thirty minute concert with the children seated on the floor in prom style, participating with the orchestra in a variety of ways, was introduced.

The selection of appropriate repertoire was clearly critical to the success of the new K-2 concerts. The programs were devised as a result of consultations with several groups. Firstly, the S.S.O. Education Officer met with the Program Advisory Group, K-2 practitioners and music educators. The teachers made general recommendations about the kinds of music their students enjoyed as well as suggesting specific works. S.S.O. management then considered the draft program with a view to practical considerations such as staging and the number of players required. Players from the orchestra were also asked for their comments on the draft program and some made suggestions about repertoire. This process of consultation with different groups took some weeks to complete.

After the initial consultation with teachers several significant issues emerged about the kind of music young children appeared to prefer. These ideas were subsequently supported by an examination of literature relating to the development of young children's musical preferences.

LISTENING PREFERENCES OF YOUNG CHILDREN

Over the past decade a number of research studies have investigated various aspects of the way children learn to listen to music. Many researchers have been concerned with finding effective ways of encouraging a liking or preference for art music, particularly orchestral music. Three main findings were influential in the choice of repertoire for the K-2 concerts.

- Musical preferences are established early in life.
  Scott (1989) states that "Research in music preference in preschoolers shows that they are open to all kinds of music and have not yet begun to form strong

preferences" (p. 30). Many studies (Peery and Peery ,1986; Bayless and Ramsey,1991; Achilles ,1992) support this view, although there is some divergence about the precise age at which preferences begin to be established. Peery and Peery (1986) found that "... young preschool children have an equal preference for popular and classical" (p. 30) and the shift to preferring popular over classical music may begin during the fifth year of life. Children's listening preferences appear to move away from what is not heard or heard infrequently. Greer, Dorrow and Hanser (1973) found no difference between the eclectic musical tastes of preschool-aged and first grade children, while Flowers (1988) found a slow decline in the popularity of symphonic music over the grades K-6 which coincided with an increased preference for popular music.

- Repetition of particular pieces or styles of music and, conversely, *not* hearing particular types of music, may be a significant influence in forming preferences. Larsen (1987) investigating the influences of home and family on the musical opportunities of educationally advantaged second-grade children, observed that in general, whatever kind of music children hear, is the kind of music that they like. Peery & Peery (1986) found that four-year-old children who received weekly lessons based on classical music over a ten month period, preferred classical music significantly more than those in a control group, who had not received those weekly lessons and who in fact declined in their liking for classical music. Peery and Peery felt that repetition, modelling and social reinforcement do influence musical preference of young children.
- Children prefer fast music to slow music.

Flowers (1988), investigating children's symphonic music preferences, observed classes from K-6. All age groups preferred fast music to slow. This finding was supported by Sims (1987) who researched the effect of tempo (speed) on the preference of children from preschool to fourth grade.

SELECTION OF ORCHESTRAL MUSIC FOR YOUNG CHILDREN

The music chosen for young audiences by the Sydney Symphony Orchestra took into account the developmental levels and characteristics of young children. The selected works were short in duration (generally about two minutes) and most pieces were fast with high energy levels. The concerts were also designed to incorporate opportunities for musical activity by the children. These activities included moving, singing and performing simple body percussion patterns (body sounds such as clapping and tapping different parts of the body) while the orchestra performed. The repertoire selected was a mix of orchestral standards, contemporary Australian works and specific children's music.

The 1992 Sydney Symphony Orchestra program for K-2 audiences was:

Shepherd's Hey	Grainger
The Little Bells (from *The Wand of Youth Suite No 2*)	Elgar
Departure (from *Winter Bonfire Op* 122)	Prokofiev

Tarantella (from *La Boutique Fatasque*)   Rossini/Respeghi
From Uluru   Sculthorpe
Bananas in Pyjamas   Blyton, arranged John.

The works by Grainger, Elgar, Prokofiev and Rossini/Respeghi are standards of the orchestral repertoire. In accord with its commitment to bringing contemporary Australian music to audiences, the orchestra commissioned composer Peter Sculthorpe to write a piece for its education program 1992. *From Uluru* resulted. An extremely popular children's song, *Bananas in Pyjamas*, was orchestrated especially for young audiences.

One other finding from the research was important in planning the K-2 program; the critical role of the teacher. Research indicates that modelling and social reinforcement by adults may be a significant influence in the formation of musical preferences of young children. The teacher may be quite significant in developing the musical preferences and listening behaviours of young children. Greer, Dorrow and Hanser (1973), Peery and Peery (1986) and Sims (1986) all found that teacher modelling can be an influence in the formation of young children's listening preferences. Acknowledging the critical role of teachers, the Sydney Symphony Orchestra Education Program personnel devised ways of assisting in preparing students for the experience of attending an orchestral concert.

SUPPORT FOR TEACHERS

In collaboration with the Department of School Education, the the Sydney Symphony Orchestra produces a teaching kit which is provided to all teachers attending the concerts. The *K-8 Teaching Kit* comprises a cassette tape of the works to be performed and a booklet of suggested music activities teachers can use in planning. The kit is written by teachers and teacher educators and is designed for generalist class teachers. A variety of activities is related to each programmed work. The activities are designed to aid teachers in helping their students become familiar with the orchestral repertoire they will experience in live performance. The kit's musical activities encourage children not only to listen to music but also to sing, move, play instruments and create their own music. The following extract is the material included for *Departure* by Prokofiev. All the activities are related to that work in some way. The activities are intended to be used as a preparation to the performance. Each activity is designed to familiarise the children with the music or to develop an understanding of a particular element of the work. The suggested activities are intended as a smorgasbord from which teachers may choose listening, singing, moving, instrumental playing or organising sound experiences that are appropriate for their class.

In addition to the kit, teachers who plan to bring their students to the concerts have the opportunity to attend a professional development day. In collaboration with a local professional association, MEIS (Music Educators in Schools), the Sydney Symphony Orchestra organises an inservice day. A series of practical workshops are presented to help familiarise teachers with the repertoire of the concerts and some of the associated teaching activities.

A local, public radio station, 2MBS FM, broadcasts programs to introduce the concert program to teachers and children. The programs include classroom activities associated with the music to be heard in concert and are presented by the Sydney Symphony Orchestra's Education officer and writers of the kit.

RESPONSE TO THE PROGRAM

In 1992, over four-and-a-half thousand children aged from five to eight years attended the Sydney Symphony Orchestra K-2 concerts. A formal review of the K-2 program is planned for 1993. Meanwhile, the response to the concerts from schools has been overwhelming, with the demand for places far exceeding those available.

Response from teachers

Teachers of children in grades Kindergarten to Year 2 are principally generalist teachers, without any specialist music training. Before the Sydney Symphony Orchestra introduced the K-2 concerts, most had not considered taking such young children to a live orchestral performance. Those that had, tended to dismiss the idea as inappropriate for their students. Notions of hour-long, inaccessible programs and restless, inattentive students dissuade them from such an undertaking.

Two factors emerged as significant for teachers in making the decision to take their classes to the K-2 programs. First was the "K-2" designation in the information sent to schools. Teachers reasoned that if the orchestra was taking the initiative of presenting concerts for this age group, they must have given careful consideration to performing for young children. "The music is specially chosen for this age group" (Christie, 1993). Some felt that the thirty- rather than fifty-minute length of the concert and the short duration of the works programmed confirmed this.

The second factor which influenced teachers to bring their students to the concerts was the *K-8 Teaching Kit*. Some teachers felt that the experience of live performance would be "almost useless without the classroom activities before the concert — The children listen better during the performance to works they know from classroom activities, because its familiar" (Guthrie, 1993). Members of the orchestra agree: "The children listen better to the pieces hey know. They have more idea how to listen, what to listen for. They concentrate better when we play." (Paige, 1993). The kit provided teachers with activities they could use to prepare their students for the performance. Teachers with a strong background in music, found that the listening, singing, moving, instrumental and creative activities suggested in the teaching kit were a helpful starting point in their planning. Often the suggested activities provided a stimulus for the teachers to

Side 1 Piece 13

Departure depicts a train journey to the country

OBJECTIVES	CONCEPT
To maintain a steady beat	Duration
To perform different rhythm patterns while maintaining a steady beat	Duration

ACTIVITIES

Performing (singing/playing/moving)

- As the student listen to *Departure*, encourage them to keep the beat of the music on their knees or by moving their arms like engine pistons.

  Note: Except for the very end of the piece, where it slows down, the tempo (speed) remains constant.

- Form students into groups of five or six to make a train. As *Departure* is played, let the trains move around the room, without collisions.

- Sing some train songs such as *Train is a-comin'*, *Four Little Engines* or *The Runaway Train*. Accompany *Departure* with the following instrumental ostinato (repeated) patterns which can be used in combination or at different parts of the piece.

    (chug chug)

    (chuff, chuff, chuff, chuff)

    (chuffa, chuffa, chuffa, chuffa)

    mm-chugga-ch-ch, mm-chugga-ch-ch)

Organising Sound

- In small groups, students use instruments or any classroom objects which can be made to sound like train sounds, Shakers, sandblocks, scrapers could be useful.

- Encourage the groups to use their sounds to make a short piece about a train-starting slowly, gathering speed, going over bridges, through tunnels, slowing down at the destination.

- Experiment with vocal sounds to simulate a train gathering speed; for example:

    | fairly slow | chug, chug, chug, chug |
    | a little faster | choo-choo, choo-choo, choo-choo, choo-choo |
    | full speed | chuffa-chuffa, chuffa-chuffa, chuffa-chuffa, chuffa-chuffa |

- Find sound sources to simulate different forms of transport such as a galloping horse, plane, sailing boat, hiker or motor bike. Compare the different sounds.

Listening

- On initial hearing of *Departure*, without telling the students the name or subject of the piece, ask them to paint or draw what they think the music is about.

- Listen for the various train sounds in *Departure* such as the train whistle, wheels moving, carriages rattling, release of steam at the end.

- Listen for how Prokofiev achieves the effect of the train starting and gathering speed.

Note: Prokofiev does not change the tempo (speed) except at the very end. The effect of increasing speed is achieved by gradually introducing shorter note values. See Performing (Activity 4) and Organising Sound (Activity 2).

Integration with other Curriculum Areas

This piece would be highly suitable for a unit on transport

Reprinted with the kind permission of the Sydney Symphony Orchestra.

design additional experiences. For teachers who felt uncertain about teaching music, the kit was also useful. "The kit provided me with a tape the music the orchestra was going to play at the concert and booklet of musical activities I could use with the children. Because music is not one of my strengths in teaching, I was glad that the kit had lots of practical ideas. I just chose the activities I felt confident with. If there were any that I didn't feel happy about, I didn't use them. I think the children in my class benefited because I was able to prepare them for the performance and some of them were so musical" (Jones, 1993).

The professional development day was also very popular with teachers, particularly the workshops on the classroom music activities in the kit. "The written word is often not as clear for teachers as actually experiencing the activity" (Christie). Similarly, "— for me, actually doing, experiencing the classroom activities gave me the confidence to try them with my class at school" (Jones).

Response from the orchestra

Playing concerts for school students can present difficulties for the orchestral musicians. The programs have particular stresses for the players associated with limited rehearsal time and performing the same program four times on the same day. Despite this, many players "realise the importance of the orchestra's education program" (Paige, 1993).

The players found that the children at the K-2 concerts were generally very enthusiastic. Some works were clearly already favourites with the children prior to the performance. 'You hear the 'oohs' and 'aahs' of recognition when the piece is announced or begins. — The little children like fast music with a strong sense of rhythm. They really liked *Departure* which is about a steam train. And *Bananas in Pyjamas* always goes down really well. They recognise it and sing along. They love it!" (Paige; 1993). The orchestra gets lots of letters from children after the concerts. Many of them write about favourite instruments or works. The youngest children seem particularly partial to trumpets and drums (Paige).

Response from the children

The children who attended the live orchestral performances found them stimulating and engrossing. Teachers reported that the experience was a very positive one for their students. "Just seeing the orchestra live is an experience in itself. — The children get more excited. It's all-enveloping for them" (Guthrie). "Their eyes light up. They're caught up in the magic of being there" (Christie). The most engaging components of the performances are those in which the children participate with the orchestra singing or clapping along; "where every child is involved" (Guthrie).

After the performance there was a good deal of talk among the children themselves and between the children and their teachers and other accompanying adults. Many children like to re-live the experience, going over what happened with their peers. "Did you see when the conductor — What about when those four musicians stood at the front and played 'Row, row row your boat' and we sang. — I liked it when that man played the big bells —"

Back in the classroom, the impact of the performance continued. Music making, art and craft, writing, dramatic play and lots of talk have all been reported. "They want to hear all the music again and do some of the music activities over again, too" (Guthrie).

However, longer term influences have yet to be assessed.

PROGRAM REVIEW

The orchestra's Education Officer believes that in 1992, the K-2 concerts "... were engaging and exciting because the children felt part of the music; actually making music with the orchestra, singing with the orchestra hearing and seeing the instruments at close quarters. The choice of repertoire was not only entertaining and exciting but extended their listening skills." (James, 1992).

The commitment of the the Sydney Symphony Orchestra to providing live performances has been expanded to include young children in the early years of school. To ensure that their K-2 program is a valuable one, the orchestra has done its best to make the concert experience developmentally appropriate by changing their performance format to meet the needs of young children rather than expecting young children to conform to adult concert-going behaviour.

A final word from a seven-year old. "It's really special at the concert. You can see the conductor and the instruments. And it's a clearer sound than the records."

References

Achilles, E. (1992) The role of parents in the development of musical behaviour in preschool children. *Australian Music Education*, 1, 22-25

Bayless, K.M. and Ramsey, M.E. (1991) *Music, a way of life for young children*. New York: Macmillan.

Christie, H. (1993, February) [Personal communication with H. Christie, K-2 teacher]

Flowers, P.J. (1988) The effect of teaching and learning experiences, tempo, and mode on undergraduates' and children's symphonic music preferences. *Journal of Research in Music Education*, 38, 102-114

Greer, R.D., Dorrow, L. and Hanser, S. (1973) Music discrimination training and the music selection behaviour of nursery and primary level children. *Journal of Research in Music Education*, 35, 30-43

Guthrie, R. (1993, February) [Personal communication with R. Guthrie, K-2 teacher.]

James, S. (1992, December) [Personal communication with S. James, Education Officer of the Sydney Symphony Orchestra.]

Johnson, B. (1990, September) [Personal communication with B. Johnson, Education Officer of the Sydney Symphony Orchestra.]

Jones, S. (1993, January) [Personal communication with S. Jones, K-2 teacher.]

Kleszynski, K. and Whiren, A. (1982) A bibliography of music for young audiences. *Childhood Education* 59(2), 120-122

Larsen, J.M. (1987) Influences of home and family on musical opportunities of educationally advantaged second-grade children. In J.C. Peery, I.W. Peery & T.W. Draper (Eds.) *Music and child development*. New York: Springer-Verlag

Paige, P. (1993, February) [Personal communication with P. Paige, violinist, Sydney Symphony Orchestra.]

Peery, J.C. and Peery, I.W. (1986) Effects of exposure to classical music on the musical preferences of preschool children. *Journal of Research in Music Education*, 34, 24-33

Scott, C.R. (1989) How children grow — musically. *Music Educators Journal*, 76(2), 28-31

Sims, W.L. (1986) The effect of high versus low teacher affect and passive versus active student activity during music listening on preschool children's attention, piece preference, time spent listening, and piece recognition. *Journal of Research in Music Education*, 34, 173-191

Sims, W.L. (1987) "Effect of tempo on music preference of preschool through fourth-grade children' in Madsen, C.K. and Prickett, C.A. (Eds.) *Applications of research in music behaviour*. Tuscaloosa: University of Alabama Press

Sims, W.L. (1990) Sound approaches to elementary music listening. *Music Educators Journal*, 77(4), 28-31

Sydney Symphony Orchestra, (1992). *1992 K-8 teaching kit*. Sydney: Australian Broadcasting Corporation

Quality children's television: the case of "Lift Off"

SUSAN E ROBERTS
Institute of Early Childhood, Macquarie University

"Lift off" is a new, innovative children's television series produced by the Australian Children's Television Foundation. It has been well received by critics, parents, educators and most significantly, by its three-to-eight year old target audience.

The program easily satisfies the five criteria for quality programming formulated by the Children's Program Committee of the Australian Broadcasting Tribunal. The typical half-hour program is dense, requiring close viewer attention but it is claimed that the viewer is rewarded for her viewing investment with an enriching and pleasurable experience. The doubt is raised that the socially disadvantaged segment of the child audience, who use television for diversion rather than enrichment, may not be prepared to make such an investment of viewing attention.

One final concern is voiced. The Foundation's official spokespeople publicly claim that "Lift Off" will enrich the lives of a whole age cohort. It is argued that such claims overemphasise the supposed direct consequences and impact of media messages on individuals.

Key words: television research, media use, television viewing, childrens television

The Australian Children's Television Foundation has produced much quality children's television in the past 10 years, but its most ambitious production to date is undoubtedly "Lift Off". The program itself is a 26 hour series aimed at three-to-eight year olds and it mixes animation, puppetry, documentary and drama. But "Lift Off" is much more than 26 hours of children's programming. It is "a national experiment. It is about integrating our two major communication institutions, television and education, for the purpose of developing the intelligences of our children through the most absorbing vehicle of all, storytelling" (Edgar 1992: 4).

Lift Off Outreach is the Foundation's organ for raising national consciousness about the program, explaining and assisting "individuals and groups to use the program in the schools, in the community and in homes" (Edgar 1992: 3). Each State and Territory in Australia has a contact person, normally in ministries of education or education faculties of universities, whose job it is to convene active community networks which disseminate information about the "Lift Off" philosophy. The New South Wales state network for example is currently developing discussion starter materials.

The Lift Off project is well funded. It is patronised by the current Australian Prime Minister's wife, Annita Keating, and was given a significant stamp of approval by the then US President's wife, Barbara Bush, in January 1992 when she visited the Foundation office. It has been sold to the British Broadcasting Commission and commences broadcasting in the United Kingdom in April. At this point, it is probably opportune to say what makes up one episode of this highly regarded program.

Brief Description and Analysis of One Episode of "Lift Off": And I Grew 2" (Broadcast originally Channel 2, Australian Broadcasting Commission, Sydney, July 1992)

The episode cuts between two major sets — a gymnasium and Poss and Nipper's flat. The narrative link between the two sets is Poss and her friend Kim's biweekly gym classes. Poss and Kim are girls of about seven, Nipper is Poss's younger brother, about three. The episode starts with the usual bright, catchy opening credits and moves straight into the witty song "And I Grew" (I did not rue, because I grew), sung by established puppet characters in the kitchen of the Wakadoo Cafe. The narrative commences at the gym with an immediate complication: Kim is now good enough to progress up to Grade 9, but she doubts she has the skill. She is held back by her fear of failure. The parallel story in Poss and Nipper's flat commences with a scene in their small bathroom and the problematic in this setting: how to share the limited bathroom facilities equitably. (Nipper wants to go to the toilet while the girls want to continue playing with makeup).

The sequence changes are numerous and each time the content of the new sequence either establishes some qualification or elaboration of the general thesis, that all living things grow; or moves the central narrative forward — Kim's progression at gym.

Some examples of the former —

(i) the well-known Australian comedian, Mark Mitchell as Seymour, inappropriately but hilariously treated like a child by Mark Mitchell reincarnated as Seymour's mother;
(ii) dialogue between two articulate girls over a largely animated sequence about the similarities between tadpole/frog, acorn/tree, child/adult;
(iii) speeded footage of baby turtles hatching and moving to the sea;
(iv) five suited comedians parodying corporate man in a wordless satire. They send up many of the hallmarks of adult life — obsession with time, correct greeting procedures, appropriate business attire.

The narrative about Kim at the gym moves towards a resolution — she finally dares to try a somersault from a high beam and succeeds. We assume she will become even more skilful as she practises and dares to succeed. She has overcome her fear of failure. But this is not the end of the episode because the parallel story with Poss and Nipper dramatises the major qualification to this success story — maturity is not just about becoming more skilful as an individual, it is also about accepting such social responsibilities as learning to share, respecting property, constraining aggression. Poss and Nipper decide that the way to avoid conflict and to live harmoniously is to abide by these few social rules. So personal maturity is more than individual growth and will to succeed, it is also about learning to live peacefully with others.

If these ideas about growth are thought to centre too exclusively on behaviour and insufficiently on attitudes and emotions, these doubts are quickly dispelled by the penultimate sequence in which the Frillseekers, the paradoxically grotty superegos of the show, laugh uproariously at the vanities of the ridiculous 2-footers. The Frillseekers are happy with the way they look, unlike the 2-footers Poss, Kim, Nipper and Seymour who worry too much about their appearance — the "outside" of themselves when the "inside" is so important. This makes sense because Kim's fear of failure drove the main narrative, and fear is clearly more than fearful behaviour. It is also a state of mind.

In all, this was a dense, demanding episode requiring close viewer attention. It followed the typical format of the show stylistically and thematically — opening song; dramatised problematic around some aspect of personal growth; mix of animation, live action, puppetry; established setting and characters; non-simplistic, satisfying resolution. The tone of the episode was lighthearted but many of the ideas stayed with this viewer long after the show finished. Links between sequences were clever, the lift doors in Poss and Nipper's block of flats often closed on an old sequence and opened on a new sequence for example. Cohesion in the episode depended on recurring locales and characters, as well as the major thematic continuity. The program as a whole looks very different from other children's television (with the exception of Sesame Street) because the pace is fast, the visual and auditory techniques are different and the ideas are challenging.

One fundamentalist Christian school on Sydney's suburban fringe has condemned "Lift Off" as over-emphasising the power of individual will at the expense of faith in God. Certainly, "Lift Off" often addresses the child's need to empower the self but this is never at the expense of the social group. It could be argued that "Lift Off's" message is consistent with Christianity, and it is certainly consistent with secular Australian culture today.

So, what is so exciting and important about "Lift Off"? In brief, the Foundation's intentions for "Lift Off" are what make it important. Outreach publications such as *The Teacher Guide to Lift Off* and *A Parent's Guide to Lift Off* advise the adult audience about the thinking behind the program, as does Boomer (1991) in an Outreach paper. "'Lift Off' is to be for all children from three to eight and will operate out of a theory that accords enormous power and capacity to young minds. The program will address children not only as if they have powerful brains but also as if those brains already have a huge scope, repertoire and potential"

(Boomer 1991: 1). The particular theory the producers chose was Howard Gardner's theory of multiple intelligences not because, as Edgar (1992: 3) is careful to point out, the series sets out to prove any theoretical perspective. Rather, Gardner's theory was chosen because it was not as age-related as say, the Piagetian position and in addition, it is less centred on cognitive development than other theories of human intelligence.

These features of Gardner's theory are important because the "Lift Off" philosophy is so wide-reaching. Boomer's key point in the introduction to the paper is a reference to "a new age of cleverness" in Australia, a direct echo of the throw-away line that became the catchcry of the 1980's — the clever country. By releasing the brainpower of the Australian young, Boomer sees "Lift Off" as an attempt at developing our nation into a cleverer one. A developmental theory which allows different children to develop through the same stages at different ages and one moreover which values aesthetic, emotional and applied intelligence as equal to cognitive intelligence, is therefore highly suited to the "Lift Off" enterprise.

Edgar (1992: 4) asks "Who knows what we may achieve as a nation if we can release and use and build on all the brainpower of the young as they begin to adventure into the world". And Boomer goes even further. He identifies "Lift Off" as an important remedy for Australia's economic difficulties by stimulating "Australian brain power" in order that we may "think our way out of trouble" (1991: 1).

This is not the first time education and children's television have been united to address socio-economic malaise. Sesame Street in the 1960's was produced by the Children's Television Workshop in New York specifically for economically and educationally disadvantaged young children in our culture. In comparison to "Lift Off", "Sesame Street's" notion of the educational curriculum was narrower. It was more concerned with fostering literacy and numeracy than other skills, but given its intentions, this was understandable. And it was not found to be successful at breaking the cycle of social disadvantage by giving educationally disadvantaged preschoolers a headstart. But it was, and remains, quality children's television, easily satisfying the criteria of the old Children's Program Committee of the old Australian Broadcasting Tribunal.

CHILDREN'S TELEVISION — THE TRIBUNAL'S STANDARDS

(a) is made specifically for children or groups of children within the preschool or the primary school age range.

The Foundation targets three-to-eight year old children, a period marked by great development in all aspects of the child-cognitive, social, emotional and physical. Does this mean that the program is insufficiently focussed on a particular age group?

Not really. It is well recognised that age seven to eight is a qualitative turning point in a child's life because by then, most children are able to decentre. That is, they are less likely to base their judgements on a single feature of an object or situation. Their thinking about objects, persons or situations is markedly different from the typically egocentric thinking of the under 8 year-old. It is no accident that 8 years of age is the commonly accepted threshold between early and middle childhood in our culture.

At about three years of age, children move away from parents towards more peer contact, and they still retain the very playful inclinations of early childhood. A television program aimed at the three-to-eight year group can assume viewer attention of more than several minutes yet should not adopt a "heavy" tone. It should dare children to attempt new tasks, play with words and ideas, dramatise fantasies and so on, if it is to deal with issues from the target child's perspective.

From the evidence of viewing the program, "Lift Off" is clearly made specifically for three-to-eight year olds. Of course, not many three-to-eight year old viewers expect television to treat their needs so seriously. Television research into the child audience has found an audience segment who rarely "give their absorbed and intense concentration to the TV screen" (Palmer, 1986, 139). Their viewing is "lively" in the sense that they play, talk and move around while they view. The child audience is rarely addressed in a demanding way in the sense that television rarely demands their full attention. "Lift Off" requires a different sort of audience response.

   (b)   is entertaining.

This is a funny, unpredictable, fast, contemporary show. It is also worthy but could never be accused of cliched writing nor poor character development, the signs of poor children's programming.

   (c)   is well produced using sufficient resources to ensure a high standard of script, cast, direction, editing, shooting, sound and other production elements.

This criterion is often interpreted to mean — how much money was budgeted for production and post-production? Certainly children's television production is notoriously underfunded so any show with a healthy production budget immediately looks different. But high production values are not just about budget, as the ABC Playschool producers would be the first to agree! It is also about talent, commitment, and time. And "Lift Off" has it all — budget, commitment and talent. Lift-Off Outreach workshop participation for example, was voluntary, but commitment was intense.

   (d)   enhances a child's understanding and experience.

This criterion is intended to separate quality programs from the mass of moving wallpaper directed at children. But as discussed at (a), many children use television in a cavalier fashion, so this criterion is vexed. Do children use television in this way because they have no choice or simply because they do not wish to use TV for the purpose of enhancement? Only longitudinal audience research can answer that question, but my guess is that "Lift Off" is likely to rate well in the long term with privileged children, and poorly with children for whom the whole notion of televisual enhancement is foreign, children whose lives are so circumscribed by constraint that the best TV can offer is distraction.

(e) is appropriate for Australian children.

Australia is an open, pluralistic society. It would be hard to reject any program on the basis of this criterion.

CONCLUDING REMARKS

Both "Lift Off" and "Sesame Street" although based on quite different educational philosophies and addressing different kinds of wider social concerns, at least share a common assumption about television. They both assume that TV is not a medium which necessarily engenders passivity in the child audience. This is a reasonable assumption. Much television programming is mind-numbingly bad, especially the television that children watch, but the medium itself may often be used creatively to provide its audience with quality programming.

My potential concern with "Lift Off", an innovative children's program, is that it should be careful about educating its audience too overtly. Boomer (1991: 1) himself describes the learning theory in-built in "Lift Off" as "clearly constructivist in orientation". In other words, the program assumes its child viewer is actively and "continually trying to make sense of the world by developing rules and concepts and then trying them out to see whether they work". Such a viewer would have little difficulty constructing the motivation behind "Lift Off", deciding if it is too educational, if it becomes school masquerading as television.

Boomer (1991: 1) also claims that "Lift Off" is a truly post-modern program in the sense of being "multi-faceted, many-layered, and culturally diverse". A viewer able to negotiate such a complex text would have no problem understanding the aims of the Foundation, should "Lift Off" offer too few pleasures.

Currently the program rates very well in its timeslot in the TV schedule. Available ratings figures are reproduced below in Table 1. It is a program which has found an audience, it is a quality program with lots of variety and visual stimulation for the young viewer. If Australia fails in its quest for cleverness in the long-term and-or fails to trade its way out of recession in the short-term, will anyone really blame "Lift Off"?

References

Boomer, G. (1991) "Lift Off to Education". *Outreach Paper* No. 4, Melbourne, Australian Children's Television Foundation
Edgar, P. (1992) "The Origins of Lift Off". *Outreach Paper* No. 5, Melbourne, Australian Children's Television Foundation
Patricia Palmer (1986) *The Lively Audience*, Sydney: Allen and Unwin

Table 1 Ratings

Time	Date	HUT	SBN/Hshlds	Ch2/Hshlds	Ch7/Hshlds	Ch9/Hshlds	Ch10/Hshlds
4.3	29.6.92 M	29	0 Close	5 Lift Off	6 Now You See It	8 Skippy	11 Wonder Years
"	30.6.92 T	25	"	7 "	6 "	5 Guess What	8 "
"	1.7.92 W	29	"	5 "	8 "	6 "	11 "
"	2.7.92 Th	26	"	6 "	7 "	5 "	10 "
"	3.7.92 Fri	26	"	6 "	6 "	4 Look Who's Talking	10 "

Key HUT = Households Using TV : Ratings do not necessarily sum to HUT because i) some households are multiset ii) some households are using VCR rather than TV. Ratings courtesy Nielsen Media Research, Sydney.

Co-player and co-artist: New roles for the adult in children's visual arts experiences

URSULA KOLBE

Institute of Early Childhood, Macquarie University

An important implication of the body of recent theory and research into children's play and children's artistic and aesthetic development, is that the role of the teacher as supportive facilitator with a hands-off, non-interventionist approach, should change. Development is fostered and learning opportunities maximised when the teacher plays a more active role within the context of the child-centred, process-oriented curriculum. This paper proposes that new understandings of children's artistic and aesthetic development be integrated with changing attitudes towards the role of the adult in children's play, particularly imaginative (fantasy) play. Suggestions are made for ways in which teachers may intervene creatively in children's artmaking, as well as extend these activities into further areas of aesthetic experience.

Key words: Visual arts, symbolisation, imaginative play, adult-child interaction

Catch phrases long associated with children's visual arts activities include "self-expression", "the process is more important than the product", and "hands-off for the teacher". Like all catch phrases which don't disappear, these hold a certain validity that is difficult to deny. Art *does* involve self-expression, the process in young children's artmaking *is* to be valued for its own sake, and a facilitative, sympathetic, non-intervening adult *is* preferable to one who directs and shapes the child's product. Nevertheless, if adhered to too rigorously, these phrases become an impediment not only to understanding what artmaking can offer the child in terms of cognitive and aesthetic development, but also to understanding the pivotal role which the teacher can play in children's artmaking.

The ideas on which this paper is based were developed during an Outside Studies Program granted by Macquarie University. I would like to thank: Macquarie University; the British Council and selected London pre-schools and schools for enabling me to see programs in action; Prof. Lois Lord, Bank Street College of Education, New York; Muriel Silberstein Storfer, Metropolitan Museum of Art, New York; and Karen Neubert, Artist in Residence, Pacific Oaks College, California, for graciously allowing me to observe their children's classes; and the University College of S. Queensland and Yvonne Winer, Child Development Unit, for inviting me to work as Visiting Artist with children.

This paper examines aspects of the teacher's role. It explores ways in which teachers may intervene creatively in children's artmaking within the context of a developmentally-based, child-centred curriculum focused on play. Some of the suggestions have been influenced by recent developments and changes that have occurred with respect to the teacher's role in children's dramatic and imaginative play. In particular, I will blend the notions of "co-player", "co-explorer", found in the literature on play (Johnson, Christie, Yawkey, 1987; Henry, 1990), with the notion of "co-artist" as advocated by Abbs (1989a) in aesthetic education. These notions will be explored in relation to the "project-approach" advocated by Katz and Chard (1990), but in the context of projects that are grounded in artmaking.

Decisions about how much or how little to intervene in children's artmaking depends on how one views and values the place of the visual arts in the curriculum. The catch-phrases mentioned above, hail from the era when art was valued primarily as a vehicle for self-expression and emotional release, and the teacher's role was seen as being essentially facilitative. This view, based on developmental and psycho-analytical theories, still informs much current early childhood practice. But today, in the light of research into children's development of representational systems, children's artmaking is also being seen as a highly significant avenue for symbol-making and the construction of meaning (Dyson, 1990; Gardner and Wolf, 1987; Golomb, 1992; Smith, 1982). Artmaking is increasingly being appreciated also as a problem solving activity, and valued for its crucial role in cognitive development. In short, artmaking is seen as a way of knowing (Abbs, 1987, p. 46).

Since the eighties, the notion that it is time for programs to go "beyond self-expression" has begun to take hold. Although the child-centred, process-oriented art curriculum is still seen as the most valuable model for early childhood art education, nevertheless it is argued that programs should promote more than the child's emotional well-being and should also actively encourage the development of symbolisation (Dyson, 1990), and aesthetic awareness (Feeney and Moravcik, 1987). The fact that researchers are currently studying how children perceive and respond to adult works of art (for example, Parsons, 1987) also has an impact on curriculum planning in the visual arts. Seefeldt (1987) suggests that the art program should provide introduction and access to the world of art as a body of knowledge in its own right. Consequently, teachers are being asked to take a more interventionist role in order to maximise cognitive and aesthetic development (Eisner, 1988; Seefeldt, 1987).

Notwithstanding these points in favour of intervention, at issue for many teachers is the reconciliation between unrestricted individual development fostered by facilitative adults (which is seen as psychologically valid), and formal learning promoted by a more interventionist approach that tends to be equated with stifling imagination and creativity. Best (1985) sees that this is a misconception of the issue. The validity of psychological arguments in favour of "free-expression" is not denied, but from a philosophical point of view, Best argues that "if certain disciplines are not acquired, whether of language, the arts, or any other subject, students are not allowed but deprived of certain possibilities for freedom of expression and individuality" (Best, 1985, p. 66).

Thus the apparent dichotomy between freedom for expression and the learning of a discipline is seen as "misconceived" (Best, 1985). This is the view of the author: that an interventionist approach is compatible with self-expression, provided that the element of play is central to the children's experiences with art media.

A dilemma for teachers is how to incorporate the demands for more content in the art curriculum while still maintaining the centrality of play. The following sections suggest ways in which teachers can assume a more interventionist role, but first it is necessary to clarify certain priorities that need to be considered in relation to planning an art curriculum.

Determining Priorities

The extent of the body of empirical investigation into children's development of representational systems, suggests that activities that encourage symbol-making and symbol-use should occupy a central position in the program. Drawing, painting (with fingers and brushes), and claywork are art forms with probably the most symbol-making potential and hence offer unlimited opportunities for children to make sense of their experienced world as well as explore imagined worlds. In contrast, programs that focus on product-centred, craft activities (with art media changing daily), or use adult-designed stencils, are unlikely to contribute to children's symbolic development. Similarly, art programs with an over-emphasis on novel sensory experiences, using materials with limited symbol-making possibilities, are unlikely to develop children's potential for symbolic play. Thus the first consideration in determining a curriculum aimed at fostering cognitive and aesthetic development should be the degree of importance and attention to be given to drawing, painting and claywork. These art forms are seen as arising from symbolic play with markmaking and shapemaking, and should be viewed as the core areas of the art curriculum. Media and tools that encourage and support the development of forms, visual order, pattern, and symbolisation should be offered. Abbs (1989b, p. 200) points out that an art medium is not "neutral", and the nature of the medium itself affects both process and outcomes — as demonstrated in Golomb's research (1974) comparing two-dimensional and three-dimensional expression. In addition to drawing, painting and claywork, other art forms such as collage, construction, printmaking, and fibrework should serve to enrich the core areas (Kolbe, 1991).

The provisioning of the environment for artmaking requires a great deal of attention if opportunities for symbolic play are to be maximised. Examples of corners set up for drawing which were "studio-like" in character, were recently seen in London and Sydney pre-schools. An area for drawing and writing (in London, appropriately named "Graphics Corner"), although not large, tended to be situated well away from general traffic, well lit, and abundantly stocked with drawing media of every kind and thickness, carefully sorted in labelled containers on shelves. Papers varying in shape, size and colour, and equipment such as scissors, staplers and adhesives, encouraged and supported every kind of drawing-writing activity that children developed spontaneously. All materials were easily accessible to children who were free to come and go as they chose. Most importantly, an interested adult was seated at the drawing table. The value of adult presence at artmaking tables cannot be overestimated as will be illustrated in the next section.

ASPECTS OF THE TEACHER'S ROLE

How can the teacher extend from what is essentially a facilitator's role to one that is more interactive? The key to appropriate intervention and participation is close, informed observation. This will be considered in the following sections under the headings of Child/Adult Interaction and Adult Intervention/Participation (although in practice, the two aspects overlap).

Child/Adult Interaction

In relation to young children's drawing experiences, Matthews (1987) insists that interaction between a child and an interested, responsive and involved adult, is essential. The interaction may at times be extremely subtle, varying between silence, running commentary, or continuous conversation between the two. Moreover, Matthews suggests that the adult should be knowledgeable enough to be able to identify the child's "conceptual concerns and provide language, materials and equipment with these conceptual concerns in mind. It means supporting and acknowledging the validity of what the child is engaging in" (p. 173).

Matthews makes an important point when he advises that the adult become aware of the child's "conceptual concerns", because only then is meaningful interaction or intervention possible. An awareness of the differences in children's styles of expression is also important as illustrated by the following anecdote which shows how symbolic play with clay developed from coil making.

Two children were seated at the clay table experimenting with making clay coils, beside an encouraging adult, also with her hands in the clay. Athena, 4 years, decided that her coil was a snake, which she proceeded to animate in an imaginative drama that involved the snake hopping onto another lump of clay (a car). It then acquired a mouse tail and journeyed through a series of gates (other lumps of clay). This drama lasted twenty-five minutes and was narrated to the teacher. Sally aged 4 years, decided her coil was a crocodile and proceeded to give it some features. Pleased with this result, she repeated her actions and made four more crocodiles, each one larger, fatter and more detailed than the last. No imaginative play ensued, but her representational skills were well extended (helped by adult verbal encouragement) and she enjoyed the experience of *arranging* the crocodiles in various configurations on the table.

The difference between the two children seems to illustrate Gardner's and Wolf's findings (1987) on the differences in children's symbolic development. Gardner and Wolf distinguish between two groups of children: one group they call "dramatists" seems compelled to develop a narrative as their primary mode for expression, whilst the other group, named the "patterners", by contrast, appears primarily intrigued by aspects of form and configurational properties, as in Sally's case. Sally's crocodiles were far more complex and developed than Athena's objects. But Athena was developing her skills as an inventor and user of symbols to represent aspects of both her experienced and imaginary world.

The teacher's interaction with each child differed, yet in both cases could be seen as interventionist. With Athena, the teacher was primarily a spectator and listener, and in a secondary role, a craftsperson, providing technical advice only when it was absolutely essential (the mouse tail kept falling off, so Athena has to learn about joining pieces of clay effectively). With Sally, the teacher acted far more as a craftsperson, appreciating the increasing detail on the crocodiles and their changing arrangements and generally encouraging Sally to develop mastery of the medium. It would have made no more sense for the teacher to expect a story from Sally, than it would have been to encourage Athena to extend her skills with clay! Importantly, each child was allowed to explore aspects that particularly interested her which was undoubtedly a factor that sustained the activity. A second factor would have been (a) the teacher's active involvement as 'co-player' with the clay initially which encouraged the children to make coils; and (b) the continued presence of the teacher aware of the children's individual "conceptual concerns".

Teachers' awareness of children's individual styles of symbolic play with art media, and knowledge of children's interests in fantasy play with art media (seen as occurring when the child integrates symbols into a creative theme or story) provides a basis for planning art projects as discussed in the next section.

Teacher-Intervention/Participation

Intervention or participation in children's play by adults as play partners taking on roles as a means to enhance skills in play, has received considerable attention since Smilansky's 1968 studies (Christie, 1985). Notions of the teacher as "co-explorer", "initiator and partner" (Henry 1990), and "co-player" (Johnson *et al.*, 1987), used in the context of children's play, suggest participatory roles which teachers might also adopt within the context of extended artwork that involves imaginative play. Such artwork is here referred to as an "art project".

Katz and Chard (1990, p. 2) define a project as "an in-depth study of a particular topic that one or more children undertake over a period of days or weeks". Katz and Chard refer to projects based mainly on topics from environmental studies; these include activities across the curriculum and often involve considerable artwork. Katz and Chard also suggest topics that are "content-free", such as colour and symmetry (p. 66), as a basis for project work. Such topics, if they remain essentially grounded in the area of the visual arts, could properly be seen as *art* projects, offering rich opportunities for artistic and aesthetic development. However, as Katz and Chard suggest, these are more likely to be "fruitful for school-age children than for preschoolers". For preschool children, I wish to highlight projects based on topics that arise out of their spontaneous images and play themes. These are likely to trigger further imaginative play which, in turn, tends to *sustain* art making. The art project may incorporate many curriculum areas, and indeed, it inevitably becomes also a literacy project when stories develop. Yet, as an art project in the first instance, it will include opportunities for the refinement of artistic skills, enhancement of perception and aesthetic awareness, as well as, when relevant, introduction to examples from the world of art. Gardner (1990) sees project work as an important part of an art program when it is (a) grounded in the arts, (b) rich in expressive possibilities and (c) meaningful to the children.

In project work both adults and children make choices and decisions. In certain art projects, particularly those of a three-dimensional nature and those closely intertwined with play, the teacher's role in developing and sustaining the project may be seen as that of "co-player" or indeed "co-artist". The notion of the teacher as "co-artist" is put forward by Abbs (1989, p. 39). Referring to primary and secondary school students, Abbs suggests that aesthetic development is enhanced through creative intervention by the teacher as "co-artist". That is, the teacher initiates aesthetic activity as well as enters it in a creative sense. (Abbs refers to the Dorothy Heathcote approach to drama as an example of creative intervention by the teacher who functions as both organiser and, at key moments, "co-dramatist"). Abbs (1987) also uses the term "co-artist" in relation to the role the teacher can play in developing students' knowledge about creative achievements of past cultures. Abb's notions will be explored here in an early childhood context with respect to project work.

Teachers should be constantly alert to possibilities for project work based on children's spontaneous images. An example of a spontaneously occurring motif that is rich in expressive possibilities is the recurring house-image. This has connotations of shelter and refuge, and seems to be a manifestation of children's apparent need to create enclosed spaces. If three-dimensional materials are offered, children will have further possibilities for creating spaces with visual complexity and variety in scale which may generate new artistic problems. Imaginative play frequently becomes interwoven with this kind of artmaking. Creative intervention by the teacher could involve structuring the artmaking environment so as to challenge children's thinking and extend their play with spatial configurations. In doing so, the teacher is making decisions of an artistic nature, and acting as both organiser and "co-artist". For instance, the teacher might provide children with a collection of cardboard grocery boxes, painted black and white for construction work. This is arguably a potentially aesthetic contribution as it will inevitably influence the appearance of the children's products. In addition to being a constructive, open-ended, non-prescriptive contribution, it is also a significant one in that the teacher is ensuring that the children's visual experience will be heightened : black and white surfaces provide an effective contrast to whatever children make or do, and thus add visual stimulation to the activity.

Assuming that such a house-making project proceeds, the teacher's role is to observe closely, anticipate needs, pose questions if appropriate, and make suggestions. Some suggestions will be technical in nature: for example in relation to the use of adhesives, or the development and refinement of skills; others are again aesthetic in character as in the selection of additional materials to meet new needs. For example, when two five-year-olds required additional materials to make a "staircase" the multi-storied house they were creating, the teacher's response depended as much on the ability to enter playfully into the pretend game, as the ability to appreciate the overall creation as an aesthetic arrangement. In other situations, where children devise their own solutions to self-generated problems, (for example, in one group, three six-year-olds devised a lift for transporting wooden people from one floor to the next in their castle) the teacher is often needed as audience member to watch children demonstrate new inventions and listen to the unfolding story.

Emergent products of a project may also prompt the teacher to introduce children to works of art which are similar in spirit to the children's own work. Gardner (1990) suggests broadening children's artistic knowledge in the context of their own artmaking. Such opportunities could include sharing reproductions, photographs, outstanding picture books (works of art in their own right), or visits to galleries and sculpture parks. In this way, project work offers ideal opportunities for introduction to the world of art, however it is important that teachers are sensitive to the 'script' that children appear to be playing. Art projects are often a blend of filtered reality and fantasy: it is essential that teachers are able to enter playfully according to children's agendas.

In a recent project focussing on three-dimensional expression through clay initiated by the writer, preschool children were introduced to the sculpture of British sculptor, Henry Moore, through a major exhibition at the Art Gallery of New South Wales, Sydney. The children were subsequently exposed to contemporary Australian sculpture in the Sculpture Park at Macquarie University. These experiences occurred in the context of the children's work with clay at preschool which had been progressing over several weeks. Factors which prompted the planning of the excursion to the Moore exhibition included the children's unflagging interest in clay as a material for making shapes and stories, and that some four year-olds were achieving self-supporting three-dimensional structures — "Look, I made mine balance!" (Sammy, 4 years 6 months).

In preparation for the excursion, a preliminary visit was made during which several facts were gleaned about Moore's artistic practice which had the potential to capture young children's imagination. Information about Moore's passion for filling his pockets with found animal bones, stones, and shells with interesting shapes, his use of unconventional tools such as a kitchen grater for texturing surfaces, and his interest in drawing the sheep in the fields near his home (featured in large photographs and drawings in the exhibition), was woven into a "story" about Moore, well before the excursion. In addition, the children were encouraged to handle sculptor's tools and to mime actions with these, as well as touch raw materials such as stone, wood, plaster, and metal. Small carvings (for example, an Eskimo soapstone animal carving) and books on Moore's sculpture were available on a low table for children to look at and touch. At the claytable, children also had opportunities to finger marrow-bones, stones and shells before working with clay. Some children made complex structures by joining bone pieces with bits of clay. By the time of the excursion, the children were familiar with terms such as "sculpture" and "chisel"

The experience in the gallery elicited a wide variety of responses from the children not only to the sculptures, which ranged in size from small pieces in glass cases to large floor pieces, but also to the drawings and photographs of lambs and sheep near Moore's studio. (See reference to "woolly" in the following transcript). The significance of the excursion for two of the children is illustrated in the following account by Scott-Mitchell (1992), which documents a subsequent child-directed play activity in the preschool.

Yesterday the children were taken to the Art Gallery of NSW to visit the Henry Moore Sculpture Exhibition.

Today during the morning play period a rug was placed on the floor. On it was a small table on which a plaster cast in the shape of an icecream container was placed.

Beside the cast were the following:
- a wooden mallet
- a kitchen grater
- a rasp
- a chisel

A cushion was placed each side of the floor.

Ben (3 years 7 months) and Kieran (3 years 7 months) approached the table.

They sat on a cushion. Ben picked up the mallet then took the chisel, said to Kieran, "We're sculpture people aren't we?" Kieran "Yeah!". He took up the rasp and pulled and pushed it across the top of the cast.

Kieran: "I'm Henry Moore, what's your name?"
Ben: "I'm Henry Moore too".
Kieran: "We're both Henry Moore".
Ben: "No we both can't both have the same name".
Kieran: "Well I'll be Henry Gore".
Ben: "That's funny, Henry Moore and Henry Gore!"

They worked on the cast for several minutes, Kieran with the rasp and Ben with the mallet and the chisel.

Ben: "I'm having a rest".
Kieran: "I'm not having a rest".
Ben: "Why don't I have a rest and you keep going".
Kieran: "We're making a funny sculpture".
Ben: "You don't hammer a file! You're not using different things".
Kieran: "I'm using the file — shall we tell the people outside what we're going to do" Hammer, hammer, hammer, bang. "Now I've hurt my finger".
Teacher: "Sometimes you hurt your fingers when you're a sculptor."

Ben continues to use the chisel and mallet digging into the top of the plaster cast.

Ben: "Oh look" — he points to an indentation that he has made on the top of the cast.

"We have to dig right"
Kieran, taking the grater: "This looks like a kitchen grater!"
Teacher: "It is. Henry Moore used lots of kitchen tools when he sculpted."
Kieran: "Mummy grates things".
Ben: "Don't grate there".

Kieran: "Now Ben, put your sculpture like that. We're making a sculpture person, a lying down one sculpture".
Ben: "No, not the lying down sculpture".
Teacher: "Which one was it?"
Ben: "The one with people standing up. We're doing the standing up one aren't we?"
Kieran: "Not like that — no we're making an eye. Don't file the eyes. Don't file it, you need to hammer it". (He's trying to gouge out the eye with the chisel.)
At this point two other children arrive.
Ben: "Jenny, my name's Henry Moore and Kieran's name is Henry Gore".
"What's this tool, it looks like a hammer"
Teacher: "Yes it looks like a hammer but it's called a mallet".
The children moved away for several minutes, but later returned to go on with their work.
Teacher: "Now Henry Moore and Henry Gore what are you making?"
Ben: "A statue standing up". (to teacher) "Were they woolly?"
Teacher: "No, I think they were smooth".
Ben: (to other teacher) "Do you want to have a big look? Sometimes we change our minds and hammer it".
This incident spanned forty minutes and took place in a very busy classroom.

Scott-Mitchell (1992) — Written observation.

The above transcript highlights the importance of follow-up experiences which enable children to make sense of encounters with the world of art through play: the children had experienced an international art exhibition, and had made it part of their world.

In summary, to further children's artistic and aesthetic development, teachers can play a vital and active role through:

- Interaction, both verbal and non-verbal. That is, teachers should observe the child working, listen to the child's commentary, identify with the problems the child sets and endeavours to solve, affirm to the child her achievements, as well as suggest ways to extend ideas if appropriate.
- Intervention/participation. As co-player and co-artist, in the context of project work based on children's spontaneous image-making, the teacher can extend expressive use of art media.
- An enriched, stimulating and challenging environment designed not only to support symbolic and imaginative play with art media, as well as artistic and aesthetic development, but which also provides encounters with the world of art.

References

Abbs, P. (1987) Towards a coherent arts aesthetic. In P. Abbs (Ed.), *Living Powers: the arts in education.* (pp. 9-65). London: The Falmer Press

Abbs, P. (1989a) *A is for aesthetic: essays on creative and aesthetic education.* London: The Falmer Press

Abbs, P. (1989b) The pattern of art-making. In P. Abbs (Ed.), *The symbolic order.* (pp. 198-210). London: Falmer Press

Best, D. (1985) *Feeling and reason in the arts.* London: Allen & Unwin

Christie, J.F. (1985) Training of symbolic play. *Early Child Development and Care,* **19**, 43-52

Dyson, A.H. (1990) Symbol makers, symbol weavers: how children link play, pictures and print. *Young Children,* **45**, (2), 50-57

Eisner, E. (1988) Structure and magic in discipline-based art education. *Journal of Art and Design in Education,* **7**, (2), 185-196

Feeney, S. & Moravcik, E. (1987) A thing of beauty: aesthetic development in young children. *Young Children,* **42**, (6), 6-15

Gardner, H. (1990) *Art education and human development.* Los Angeles. CA: The Getty Centre of Education in the Arts

Gardner, H. & Wolf, D. (1987) The symbolic products of early childhood. In D. Gorlitz & J. Wohlwill (Eds.), *Curiosity, imagination and play,* (pp. 305-325), Hillsdale, NJ: Erlbaum

Golomb, C. (1974) *Young children's sculpture and drawing: a study in representational development.* Cambridge, MA: Harvard University Press

Golomb, C. (1992) *The child's creation of a pictorial world.* Berkeley & Los Angeles, CA: University of California Press

Henry, M. (1990) More than just play: the significance of mutually directed adult-child activity. *Early Child Development and Care,* **60**, pp. 35-51

Johnson, J.E., Christie, J.F., Yawkey, T.D. (1987) *Play and early childhood development.* Glenview, Illinois: Scott, Foresman & Co

Katz, L. & Chard, S.C. (1990) *Engaging children's minds: the project approach.* Norwood, N.J.: Ablex Publishing Corp

Kolbe, U. (1991) Planning a visual arts program for children under 5 years. In S. Wright (Ed.), *The arts in early childhood.* (pp. 25-51). Sydney: Prentice Hall

Matthews, J. (1987) The young child's early representation and drawing. In G.M. Blenkin & A.V. Kelly (Eds.), *Early childhood education: a developmental curriculum.* (pp. 162-183). London: Paul Chapman

Parson, M. (1987) *How we understand art: a cognitive developmental account of aesthetic experience.* Cambridge, U.K.: Cambridge University Press

Scott-Mitchell, C. (1992) Written free play observation, Child & Family Study Centre, Institute of Early Childhood, Macquarie University, May 13, 1992

Seefeldt, C. (1987) The visual arts. In C. Seefeldt (Ed.), *The early childhood curriculum: a review of current research.* (pp. 183-210). New York: Teachers College Press

Smith, N.R. (1982) The visual arts in early childhood education: development and the creation of meaning. In B. Spodek (Ed.), *Handbook of research in early childhood education.* (pp. 295-317). New York: Free Press

Empowering children through drama

KATHLEEN WARREN

Institute of Early Childhood, Macquarie University

The theatre has long been a powerful medium which enables human beings to examine their world and the people who inhabit it with them. Through drama people can learn more about themselves and others and can develop a greater understanding of society. Drama in education allows children to follow the same path of discovery. Drama facilitates the transfer of power from adults to children in developmentally appropriate ways.

This article explores the process of experiential drama in which adults and children work together and in which this transfer of power is engendered.

Key words: experiential drama, mantle of the expert, metaxis, power, teacher in role, scaffolding the learning

DRAMA AS AN EMPOWERING MEDIUM

In modern western societies, young children have little real power. Their lives and activities are governed by older and more powerful human beings. Yet learning to take control over our own lives is a crucial developmental task for all people. It is important, therefore, for early childhood educators to consider safe and appropriate ways of transferring power from adults to children.

Drama provides an excellent vehicle through which power can be transferred to children in ways that are developmentally appropriate. Children can make choices, resolve difficult issues, make decisions, and solve problems which will contribute substantially to the course of a drama experience. The co-operation engendered, what Neelands (1984: 24) calls the teacher-learner partnership in drama, provides the requirements for a truly co-operative undertaking in that the children are able to negotiate and work with others towards a mutually satisfying goal (Goffin, 1987).

In a drama experience, the children can decide what will happen and when; they can own the drama in ways that are both safe and productive and can feel their part in the drama is of the utmost importance as they are led towards influencing "the thoughts, feelings, expressions and creative outcomes" which develop (Arnold, 1991: 19).

WHAT IS DRAMA?

A comprehensive definition of drama is presented by Clark and Goode (1991: 10):

The dramatic process is practical, immediate and engages both the emotions and the intellect. The essential feature of the dramatic process is that participants are asked (a) to step out of their real situations and roles and (b) to project themselves into imagined situations and roles. This action is shared by and with a group of others. So drama occurs when a group agree to pretend and maintain that pretence in action through the imagined use of people, time and space.

This definition can apply to drama in all its forms, from a full scale professional production in a theatre, to a drama experience planned for and implemented with two-year-olds in a child care centre. Drama has its beginnings in the dramatic play of children and Fein's (1987) definition of socio-dramatic play, cited in Dau (1991: 72) shows drama's links with play very clearly.

In pretend play one object is used as if it were another, one person behaves as if she were another, and an immediate time and place are treated as if they were otherwise or elsewhere.

Early childhood educators can use children's existing experiences of play as a basis for drama so their learning can be both focussed and deepened (Neelands, 1984). Anim-Addo (1990) suggests that, when left to themselves children's dramatic play will not take those children beyond what they already know. In a carefully planned and effectively implemented drama experience children can and do go beyond what they already know.

Wheeler (1991: 11) regrets that dramatic play is often considered to be "an evolutionary process" through which all children should pass as they progress to more formal education. Early childhood educators who realise the value of play and of drama experiences in helping children learn will be anxious to build further on these foundations.

Drama, like play (Atkins, 1981) stimulates creativity and imagination through the cognitive processes of observing, experimenting and problem solving. Hill and Reed (1990) refer to the importance of developing social competence in children. Skatowski (1992) extends this view, claiming that drama can be a powerful educational tool. By bringing together historical knowledge, communicative knowledge, critical knowledge and aesthetic knowledge it develops what Skatowski (1992: 23) calls "humanistic competence".

The approach to drama that will be discussed in this article is not focussed on the child as performer. It does not concern itself with a *product* to be shown to an audience, even a friendly and familiar audience of other children in the school or centre. Rather is it concerned with the *process* of developing an experiential drama in which children and adults work together and in which children are able to identify with imagined roles and situations and through this identification and interaction, explore issues, events and relationships (O'Neill and Lambert, 1982). Thus, experiential drama can be an enabling process for children.

THE LEARNING PARTNERSHIP

Children and adults take roles in a drama. Together they influence the story's path, and ultimate conclusion, face and overcome difficulties, solve problems that arise as the drama progresses and make decisions which will determine its course. In other words, they *experience* all that occurs.

Drama enables children and adults to interact and co-operate in partnership with each other. All are equal and all are involved in the development of the drama (Warren, 1992). As Neelands (1984) points out, drama implies that the adults who are taking part do not know everything but are as interested in finding new understanding and insight as are the children. The realigning of relationships which occurs when adults negotiate for a change in the power structure enables children to draw on their own powers, the emergence of which, in other circumstances may not be encouraged (Heathcote, 1978).

An example of this was observed in a drama in which a group of pre-schoolers were in role as ghosts who were looking for somewhere to live. They approached resident householders (adults in role) asking if they could move into the houses. The householders (each adult played two or three householders, in turn) refused them entry giving a variety of excuses. One said she already had a family of ghosts living in her attic and there was no room for any more. Another asked what sort of accommodation they were looking for and when the ghosts replied that they were looking for an attic, this householder said she was very sorry but her house did not have an attic. The task facing the children then, was to consider and implement alternate solutions.

In another drama, a group of astronauts (the children in role) built a space ship and visited a faraway planet where they met an unpleasant character (an adult in role) who plotted to steal the spaceship. The children, therefore, in the role of astronauts, had to argue and negotiate their way out of the dilemma and eventually foil the would-be thief.

PLANNING A DRAMA EXPERIENCE

As with all learning experiences, careful planning by the teacher is essential. Yet at the same time, the drama must be structured so as to allow input from the children. The two are not mutually exclusive. An early childhood educator in planning a drama experience needs to decide a) objectives for the lesson, b) the topic around which the drama will be woven, c) the focus or problems to be presented, d) the ways in which those problems will arise and e) either decide or have some idea of the roles which may be played by both adults and children. Many of the details of the story line and of the actions of the characters in the drama can safely be left to the children to decide on as the drama progress.

As Wagner (1976) points out, planning needs to occur before the lesson and during it. For example, a teacher in role as someone who needed a magic carpet asked a group of pre-schoolers (cast as giants) where they thought one could be found. They suggested there was a magic carpet on the top of a high mountain. The teacher then had to decide how to handle that information and how to introduce the next phase of the experience. Thus planning occurs spontaneously as the lesson progresses and in response to the children's ideas and suggestions.

At all times, teachers need to be ready and able to put the children's needs before their own plans (Heathcote, 1969). This is what empowers the children as they see their own ideas function effectively. It does not imply that the children should be allowed to run riot. An effective drama experience is not one in which the children are left to their own devices, taking complete control and developing the activity at will. As Warren (1992) points out, this approach is doomed to failure. Even if disorganised chaos does not result, the children will have been denied the opportunity to extend their knowledge and understanding.

The following account provides an example of how a teacher, through planning both before the lesson began and again during it, was able to forestall and so prevent the situation getting out of hand. The teacher was in role as a photographer who had been commissioned to take some underwater shots and the children had been cast as marine biologists whose professional advice the photographer needed.

While under the sea, the children were asked who they would like to meet and they decided on a mermaid. Another adult took the part of the mermaid and the children coached her in movement and behaviour appropriate for such a creature. The mermaid swam up to the group and demanded to know their business. The children, in the role of the marine biologists explained and asked the photographer to show the mermaid the camera. She did and the mermaid immediately snatched it and swam off. (This action on the part of the mermaid had been planned by the teacher before the lesson began. If the children had chosen to meet some other sea creature, it would have reacted in the same way.)

At this stage of the lesson, the teacher in role as the photographer realised that unless she acted to prevent it, the children might well chase after the "mermaid" and physically overpower her. This would not constitute an appropriate transfer of power and must be circumvented before it occurs. Having realised the possible consequences, the teacher in role as the photographer, had sat the children down before the mermaid snatched the camera. Therefore, when the theft occurred it was easy for the photographer to say, "Let's all sit very still and watch where she goes". When the mermaid sat down at the other end of the room and began to examine the camera, the photographer was able to say "Let's just listen carefully and see if she says anything." However, had the children been standing when the camera was taken, it would have been too easy for them to run after the mermaid before the teacher was able to prevent it.

The teacher, still in role as the photographer was then able to ask the children for the ideas as to how the camera could be regained. Any suggestions that involved chasing after the mermaid were met with doubtful concern. "Well, I've heard that mermaids can swim faster than any human being and I don't want her to swim off where we can't find her." or "But she knows the sea so much better than we do and she could swim off and hide somewhere we would not know about." The teacher realised that it was important to accept the children's initial simplistic suggestions but to counter them in such a way as to encourage further consideration of the problem.

Although requiring surefootedness and quick thinking, a teacher in role can elicit as many suggestions from the children as they are able to give and can ask questions which draw on children's knowledge of under the sea geography and life and their expertise as marine biologists. Eventually the group can decide upon a course of action that will lead to the return of the camera. Thus the children, in their roles as marine biologists, will have solved the problem and the teacher will have facilitated this process.

DRAMA AND THE ZONE OF PROXIMAL DEVELOPMENT

Heathcote (1985) believes that children have much knowledge and understanding that is not recognised by either the children themselves or the significant adults in their lives. Drama (Warren,1992) can act as a catalyst that can unearth this knowledge and understanding which will then be of use to its owners and this is most likely to occur if the children are framed in a position of influence within the drama context (Heathcote, 1984).

Vygotsky (1978) writes of the zone of proximal development whereby, with assistance, children can solve problems they could not solve alone, given their level of actual development. Drama builds on the zone of proximal development by putting children in touch with their current knowledge and understanding at whatever level it may be. At the same time it introduces new experiences, new skills, and new knowledge and understanding all of which serve to further empower children (Juliebo, Thiessen and Bain, 1991).

Bruner (1988) uses the term scaffolding to describe the teacher's role in extending and developing children's knowledge of the world. Simons (1991) believes that drama does this when children are engaged in a fictional context which draws on their knowledge of the real world. Children are put into a drama situation in which they have to consider and act upon a problem that arises in the course of the drama. As they communicate with others, they are let towards a solution to the problem and at the same time to an increased understanding of the situation.

An example occurred in a drama experience in which a group of six-year-olds in role as explorers, had discovered, at the back of a deep cave, a creature (an adult in role) which was unique and which had long been assumed to be extinct. The teacher, also an explorer, but now in the role Morgan and Saxton (1987: 45) have referred to as "devil's advocate", took the children aside and suggested that there would be a lot of money to be made if the creature could be persuaded to return with the group to civilisation where it could be on show.

The children were aghast at the suggestion and expressed a much greater understanding of the issues concerning endangered species than might have been expected of six-year-olds. The children were able to do as Vygotsky suggested they could; they were able to externalise internal knowledge that they certainly possessed and through this externalisation, were able, immediately, to take conscious control of that knowledge.

As the drama progressed, the children and teacher, still in role as explorers, left the creature in its cave and returned to a farm nearby where, at an earlier stage in the drama, they had decided to leave their horses while they explored the nearby cave systems. The farmer (another adult in role) met them cheerily and chatted about the weather and the horses before asking casually, "And where did you go from here? Did you get to see those caves you were talking about when you left the horses here?" The children immediately became wary but agreed that they had explored the caves nearby.

The farmer went on, "Anything interesting in any of them?" The teacher still in role as one of the explorers and still playing the part of devil's advocate, said "I suppose we could tell the farmer what we found." The children immediately refused and expressed again their concern and their knowledge and understanding of endangered species.

This example indicates how a teacher was able to scaffold a lesson so that the children were able to draw on internal knowledge and understanding and externalise it to facilitate the development of new and more complex concepts, an empowering process indeed. The cues to which the children have to attend in order to facilitate this externalisation are provided by the drama structures set up by the teacher. As Simons (1991) points out this maximises the learning potential of the experience.

FRAMING CHILDREN IN A POSITION OF INFLUENCE: MANTLE OF THE EXPERT

To frame children in a position of influence, it is necessary to consider the role/s to be taken in a drama experience by both adults and children. For adults, working in role enables them to use a powerful tool that enables a drama to be elevated to a higher and more complex learning experience (O'Neill, Lambert, Linnell and Warr-Wood, 1976). For children, the roles they adopt can allow them to assume expertise that is essential for the drama to progress.

Heathcote has coined the phrase "mantle of the expert" to describe the situation in which the children are cast in a role and set upon a task that demands they function as experts (Heathcote, 1984). It is this expertise that the teacher, also in role, needs. Warren (1992) has discussed the areas in which young children can be regarded as experts and the list is extensive. Children can be cast as experts in any area in which they have any knowledge at all. It does not have to be comprehensive knowledge although adults are more likely to underestimate than overestimate the knowledge and understanding of young children.

While there may be occasions when children are best cast as people who happen to be around, Warren (1992) suggests that it is more empowering to cast children as adults who have some specific expertise. The children's status can be enhanced if they are continually referred to by their correct title as follows: "I do hope you marine biologists will be able to tell me what I could take photos of if I go under the sea." or "I want to plan a garden that will attract birds and so I have come to you ornithologists for help."

TEACHER IN ROLE: CHILDREN IN ROLE

The roles to be taken by adults and children will, of course, be determined by the subject of the drama. If the drama is to be based on a story with which the children are familiar, appropriate roles may be fairly obvious although the characters to be played by either adults or children need not be characters who appear in the original story although they should be characters who could have been a part of such a story. For instance the characters in the story of *Three Billy Goats Gruff* the characters are the three billy goats and the troll. In a drama experience the children could be cast as farm workers who cannot understand why the billy goats have not come across the bridge as they usually do and set off to investigate.

If the drama is to be planned around some issue or topic of interest to the children, there will be many possible roles depending on the ways in which the subject is to be approached. There is scope then for embellishing and extending the roles to be taken rather than using roles which are already established. If, for example, the teacher wanted to engage the children in a drama about the preservation of forests, the children could be cast as forest rangers who meet an adult in role as someone who wants to cut down the trees.

The children, in their roles, have the task of dissuading this person. Perhaps the children could be cast as botanists who are journeying to the forest to catalogue the varieties of trees to be found there and meet someone (an adult in role) who is in some way set upon the destruction of the natural environment.

Another means of transferring power to children within a drama experience may be to ask the children to decide on the role to be taken by an adult. Bolton (1984) describes a lesson in which a group of five year olds decided that the teacher should take the role of a wicked witch. They then had to instruct the teacher in ways of moving, speaking and behaving that were appropriate for a witch. In other words, the children were given the task of *creating* the character. Such role-playing can offer exciting and innovative sequences.

Adults can take role of high medium or low status (Neelands, 1984; Morgan and Saxton, 1987). If the aim is to empower children, a high status role is probably the least useful (Warren, 1991). A low or medium status role will enable children to contribute ideas, to make decisions and to suggest solutions to problems that arise in the drama and which can be followed as the drama proceeds. In other words, such a role will be more empowering of the children.

THE MATERIAL AND THE FOCUS OF DRAMA

Adults who are not experienced in drama may think first of getting children to act out stories they have heard. This is a limiting exercise and can create a dichotomy between active and passive participation on the part of the children. It does not facilitate the transfer of power which is so valuable (Warren, 1992).

If, however, adults use well known stories as starting points, beginning with an incident from the story or an incident which could have been in the story or perhaps a character from the story or a character who could have been in the story, the opportunities for original and creative involvement by all the children are increased. As Bolton (1984) points out, drama is less concerned with the sequential actions of a plot or story than it is with the emotions and the interactions that are being developed by both children and adults.

Heathcote (1967) writes:

> Drama is not stories retold in action. Drama is human beings confronted by situations which change them because of what they must face in dealing with those challenges. An open ended situation is easier for teachers who feel themselves to be novices than a story where the beginning and the end are pre-known.
>
> Johnson and O'Neill, (1984: 48)

When planning drama experiences for young children, the early childhood educator makes a decision about the topic of the drama. Suitable topics have been suggested by Davies (1983) and Warren (1992) elaborates on this and discusses suggestions in detail.

Wagner (1976) recommends using the knowledge, feelings and experiences that human beings have in common, regardless of their culture, social status and age as bases for drama experiences. Thus children can be led to consider, through drama, the relationships that lie between people. A drama based on the kitten who lost her mittens, for example, is about how people feel when their property is lost and the steps they may take to regain it. From there it is a short step to considering what to do with property that is not yours.

Rosen (1982) offers numerous examples of everyday knowledge and cultural resources which can be used as bases for drama experiences, claiming that these encompass knowledge about which all children, regardless of ethnicity, cultural, social or family background. age or ability, have, at least in part, some knowledge and understanding. Early childhood educators' understanding of the developmental needs and levels of the children in their care will help them decide on drama topics that are relevant to the children with whom they work.

Along with decisions about topics come decisions about focus which can also be defined as the problems or issues that arise in the drama. This is a determining factor in the drama's progress (Davies, 1983) Drama that does not present a problem to be resolved is unlikely to be effective drama (Warren, 1992). Stentiford (1985: 21) elaborates:

(focus) . . . is used for belief building throughout the lesson; it defines the moment; highlights the problem; controls the situation; concentrates the group's attention; exposes the contradictions within the drama; elevates the individual statement; rebuilds confidence and finally adds impact to the drama.

If an effective focus has been decided upon and if the children have been framed in a position of influence and are cast in roles which demand their expertise, the drama is well set to enable the transfer of power to occur. A problem has been presented which the children, with the expertise that has been attributed to them, will progress towards solving.

DRAMA IS FICTIONAL

It is important that children know that the drama in which they will become involved is fictional. It is impossible for power to be transferred to children if they are worried about whether the situation is real or imaginary. No transfer of power will occur if children remain in a state of ambiguity. All their energy will go into trying to resolve this by asking questions such as ones which were asked by children as drama experiences were introduced. "Are we really going to the moon?" asked a little girl concernedly. "I don't want to be someone else, I want to be Jake." said Jake firmly. These children were only able to involve themselves in the drama when other children pointed out "We are only pretending."

Part of transferring power involves the adults in making it quite clear that the group will be engaged in an imaginary undertaking, "being and doing in an imaginary context," (Parsons, Schaffner, Little and Felton, 1984:9). While most young children have no difficulty in understanding and accepting the fictional nature of a drama experience, a few may need the information to be repeated and reinforced throughout the drama as the following example shows, "Yes, usually I am Pat, but in our drama today I am Red Riding Hood's mother."

The teacher can choose to stop the drama while a particular point is clarified. This does not destroy children's belief in the story they are creating, but strengthens it. As Baker and Cross (1991) point out, stopping a drama experience and allowing children to discuss and come to terms with its inner workings, is an empowering experience. The children know that they are in charge.

An example of this occurred in a lesson in which the children were in role as firefighters and the teacher as a new recruit to the fire brigade. The teacher in this role began by asking the experienced fire fighters what their work entailed and by using questions and comments to extend their thinking while still in the role of the new recruit. After this discussion had continued for a while and the teacher in role decided it was time to move on, a previously arranged signal was given by the teacher to another adult who rushed into the scene saying that there was a fire and the fire fighters were needed.

Here the teacher stepped out of role and asked the children if they would like to be the fire-fighters who put out that fire. They agreed. They had already mentioned the need for fire-fighters to have a fire-engine, so the teacher suggested that they build the vehicle out of chairs. This building of equipment or scenery within a drama serves to strengthen the children's commitment to the experience. They decide how the fire-engine is to be built and so are able to feel that it is their own creation.

Later in this same drama, at the scene of the fire, the teacher, back in role as the new recruit asked what would happen if someone was trapped on the top of a building that was on fire. From there it was a small step to ask the children if they would like that to happen in the drama and when they agreed. an adult was chosen for the role. The children suggested she stand on a table and gave her some appropriate lines and actions. She had to wave her arms and cry "Help! Help!" The *children* set up the situation; it was of their own making. By stopping the drama the teacher was able to transfer the responsibility for deciding how the drama should progress to the children.

Drama requires us to hold the real world and the fictional one in mind at the same time. Augusto Boal called this process "metaxis". Young children are able to achieve this "heightened state of consciousness" (Boal, 1979) just as older children and adults are, and this ability in itself is empowering.

In a drama experience with pre-schoolers an adult was in role as Red Riding Hood's mother and was upset over the fact that her daughter appeared to have been lost in the woods. The children were in role as search and rescue people who had been brought in to help find Red Riding Hood. It was necessary for the teacher to stop the drama to introduce another character. Red Riding Hood's mother had been crying softly as the search continued but as soon as the teacher said "Let's just stop the drama for a minute" a child turned to the adult in role and said "You can stop crying now." Stepping outside the drama for a moment or two gives children real power over what is happening and also serves to strengthen their involvement.

After establishing the topic and the focus of the drama, and casting both adults and children in roles which enable the children to assume the "mantle of the expert", early childhood educators need to consider how a drama can progress so power continues to be ascribed to the children. In the roles the children have taken they will be asked to provide the information and suggestions for action that will ultimately lead to the resolution of the problems and issues presented.

QUESTIONING AND RESPONDING

Questioning is fundamental to the transfer of power in drama experiences. The questions asked of the children help establish the fictional context, move the drama along, challenge children and encourage their use of expressive language (Parsons, 1991). Questioning serves to transfer power from adults to children and this is most likely to occur when the questions asked are one to which the adult does not appear to know the answer. As Morgan and Saxton (1987) point out, there are two elements of questioning to be considered.

Firstly, questions should be phrased in ways that will tap into children's knowledge and experience and secondly, the questioner must be able to handle the answers. Questions must be asked as if the questioner really wants to know the answer, not as if he or she is testing to see if the children do. No transfer of power will occur if children feel they are being tested and if the adult asks questions which suggest there is a correct answer which the children are expected to provide.

A drama lesson began by an adult wearing what was fairly obviously a witch's costume entering the scene. She had previously donned it in full view of the children. To suddenly appear in such a costume could be frightening to young children. Dressing in front of them, especially if they hand over the costume or even help the character dress gives them immediate power over the character for they have help to create it.

When the adult re-entered, the teacher asked in astonishment, "Whoever could this be?" When a group of developmentally disabled children decided she was "a star lady" the teacher accepted this and a star lady she became. On another occasion a three year old group decided the character was "the magic woman of the mountains". When teachers accept children's suggestions they liberate both adults and children. New possibilities open to the adult and the act of identifying and naming the character empowers the children.

Other examples of questions which do not restrict the children's responses are taken from drama lessons carried out with pre-schoolers. "What sort of a dance could we perform at Cinderella's wedding?" was asked of entertainment consultants (pre-schoolers, in role) who were being hired to plan the entertainment at the wedding of Cinderella and the prince. "I'm new to the job," said an adult in role as a new recruit to the police force, "and they told me I would have to go into kindergartens and talk to children but I don't know what I should tell them. I thought if I came to see you (children in role as experienced police officers) you would be able to give me some ideas."

Parsons, Schaffner, Little and Felton (1984) conducted research which led them to conclude that questions that asked "why?", "what would happen if" or which focused on human feelings about an issue were particularly useful questions in encouraging thought and language. Although the initial research was conducted with ten year old children, the principle is applicable to any age. These questions are particularly useful in empowering children. They enable children to use and hence to develop higher order language and complex skills of reasoning.

"What would happen if Santa did not get his sleigh back?" was asked in a drama experience in which pre-schoolers were cast as detectives who were investigating its disappearance. "Why would anyone want to steal Santa's sleigh, I wonder?" "I wonder what the children would think if Santa could not get around at Christmas." These are all questions to which there is no correct answer. The children are empowered to consider the issues posed and to explain the circumstances according to their own ideas and understanding for questions in drama are concerned with the *issues* that surround the drama's focus (Morgan and Saxton, 1991).

However, if the asking of questions is important, so are the ways in which educators respond to the children's responses. Children are empowered if their responses are taken seriously whether or not they are acted upon at that moment. To ask for children's opinions and advice is empowering in itself. Early childhood educators do not need to follow every suggestion as it occurs. If it is accepted with respect and as if it forms a valuable contribution to the discussion, children will feel that what they have said has been valued.

Drama experiences often involve children in travelling from one place to another. "I don't know where we should go to start to look for the Batmobile," says a teacher in role as someone who has been commissioned to find detectives who could solve the mystery of its disappearance. Obviously children will make several suggestions. It is the adult's role to reflect back these suggestions and to encourage the children to make a decision.

In one lesson where the focus was on the return of the lost Batmobile, the detectives eventually decided that they should travel to a castle in the sky which was where they believed they would find the thief and eventually the Batmobile. The teacher in this drama had not specified that the Batmobile had been stolen, she merely reported that it was missing. The children had added this dimension. Once the destination was decided upon, the teacher asked "Well how do we get there" Again, several ideas were produced. The teacher repeated each one seriously and as if it was an excellent suggestion, but the ideas were many and varied, so she then asked, "Well which would be best do you think" thus helping the children to work towards consensus.

If adults who work with children are used to asking questions to which they believe there is a preferred answer, the discipline involved in accepting children's responses as if they are valued contributions can be challenging. The technique is well worth perfecting however, for the empowerment of children that results not only contributes to the drama itself but also develops a confidence in children and a belief that what they have to say is worthwhile. As Parsons (1991) says it helps build their belief in themselves as competent and capable people. It also serves to keep teachers genuinely interested in the children's ongoing learning. An early childhood teacher education student made this comment on one of her first drama experiences:

I found myself being truly curious as to what the children were going to tell us ... I felt as though they were narrating a story to me and all I had to do was ask the right questions to have the satisfaction of finding out the conclusion of the story. (Pharo, 1992)

In terms of the drama's progression, it may not matter what the children suggest as they solve the problems that have been presented to them in the drama. "How shall we get to the dark, dark wood?" some children were asked. The suggestions included walking, motor-bikes, a bus, a helicopter and an aeroplane. From the teacher's point of view any of these would have been acceptable.

"She said she wants shoes that will take her a long way," said a teacher in role as the proprietor of a shoe shop referring to another adult who was in role as a customer. The children were in role as shoe manufacturers to whom the shopkeeper had come for advice as to the best type of shoes for the customer's purpose.

Here, the teacher needs to consider the answers in terms of their potential. "I mean, where would she be going if she wanted to go a long way?"

The answers included Disneyland, to Nana's place, to the beach, to the North Pole, to the top of a high mountain and to an island. An adult who receives these suggestions recognises that not all the alternatives are equally valuable. Disneyland and Nana's place are limiting in what they can offer the children as the drama progresses, but the other suggestions have lots of promise. The teacher can simply say, as if also trying to work out the problem, "Well if she needs special shoes, she must be going somewhere where her ordinary shoes won't do. Do you think it is the North Pole, or an island or to the top of a high mountain?"

Once the children have agreed on a destination, the shopkeeper can send the shoemakers over to the customer to check if they are right. Of course, they will be! The next question to be asked (and here the expertise of the shoemakers comes into its own) will be, "Well what sort of shoes should she wear if she is going to the North Pole?" This is where the adult in role as the shopkeeper may have show restraint. If the children are convinced that party shoes are what will be required, the shopkeeper can say, doubtfully, "Are you sure? They do say it gets very cold at the North Pole" and so try to extend the children's thinking.

If the children cannot be swayed, however, their suggestion must be accepted, for after all it is their expertise that the adult in role as the shopkeeper has come to elicit. Another question could be asked. "Do you have special party shoes that will keep people's feet warm? What are they like?" The shoemakers' expertise then continues to be to be respected and the children are led to some imaginative and innovative thinking.

CONCLUSION

Early childhood educators recognise the importance of enabling children to experience power in appropriate ways. However, allowing children to take too much power is detrimental to their development as it enables them to manipulate and alienate others (Pena, French and Holmes (1987). This sort of power is, of course, developmentally inappropriate.

Pena et al. (1987) discuss ways of transferring power so young children can develop a sense of autonomy. They consider appropriate the provision of choices, the encouragement of self-help skills and the properly supervised and directed use of adult tools and materials. They also believe that children's understanding of power can be extended if the significant adults in their lives use the terms "power" and "powerful" as they describe children's actions, decisions and ideas.

All of these techniques can be successfully incorporated in a drama experience but drama's role in empowering children is due in no small part to its ability to ascribe expertise in any given area through the powerful techniques of teacher in role and mantle of the expert.

Drama and theatre have long been amongst society's most powerful instruments in allowing people to examine and understand themselves, the world and the place of human beings in that world (Harwood, 1984). Perhaps that is why there have been many attempts to control or outlaw it by church and state (Skatkowski, 1992) throughout the world and throughout history as they have feared its power (Wilson, 1985). Drama in education is also an empowering medium as it allows children to use this art form to develop their own understanding of their world.

References

Anim-Addo, J. (1990) Moving from story to drama with nursery children. *London Drama*. March, 14–15
Arnold, R. (1991) *Drama in the round: the centrality of drama in learning*. Sydney: Educational Drama Association of NSW
Atkins, J. (1981) Is play quite the thing? in *Times Educational Supplement*. September 25
Baker, L. and Cross, D. (1991) First steps in drama. *The J. for Drama/Dance in Education*. 11(1), 18–27
Boal, A. (1979) *Theatre of the Oppressed*. London: Pluto Press
Bolton, G. (1984) *Drama as Education*. London: Longman
Bruner, J. (1988) Vygotsky: a historical and conceptual perspective. in N. Mercer (ed.) *Language and Literacy from an Educational Perspective*. London: Open University Press
Clark, J. and Goode, T. (1991) On a road to nowhere. *The Drama Magazine: J. of National Drama*. July. 10
Davies, G. (1983) *Practical Primary Drama*. London: Heinemann Educational
Fein, G. (1987) Pretend play: creativity and consciousness. Cited in E. Dau (1991) Let's pretend: socio-dramatic play in early childhood. in S. Wright, (ed.) *The Arts in Early Childhood*. Sydney: Prentice Hall
Goffin, S. (1987). Co-operative behaviours: they need our support. *Young Children*. January. 75–81
Harwood, R. (1984) *All the World's a Stage*. London: Methuen
Heathcote, D. (1967) Improvisation. in L. Johnson and C. O'Neill (1984). (Eds.). *Dorothy Heathcote: Collected Writings on Education and Drama*. London: Hutchinson
Heathcote, D. (1969) Dramatic activity in L. Johnson and C.O'Neill (1984). (Eds.). *Dorothy Heathcote: Collected Writings on Education and Drama*. London: Hutchinson
Heathcote, D. (1978) Excellence in teaching. in L. Johnson and C. O'Neill (1984) (Eds.). *Dorothy Heathcote: Collected Writings on Education and Drama*. London: Hutchinson.
Heathcote, D. (1984) Dorothy Heathcote's notes. in Johnson, L. and O'Neill, C. (Eds.). *Dorothy Heathcote: Collected Writings on Education and Drama*. London: Hutchinson.
Heathcote, D. (1985) *Personal Tutorials with Dorothy Heathcote*. Newcastle-upon-Tyne. (Based on discussions by the author with Heathcote and unpublished.)
Hill, T. and Reed, K. (1990) Promoting social competence at preschool: the implementation of a co-operative games program. *Early Child Development and Care*. 59, 11–20
Juliebo, M., Thiesses, J., and Bain, B. (1991). Drama: the perfect lure. *The Drama Magazine: J. of National Drama*. March. 7–8
Morgan, N. and Saxton, J. (1987) *Teaching Drama: A Mind of Many Wonders*. London: Hutchinson
Morgan, N. and Saxton, J. (1991) Well if I called the wrong number, why did you answer the 'phone? *Drama Contact*. Autumn, No. 15. 13–15
Neelands, J. (1984) *Making Sense of Drama*. London: Heinemann Educational
O'Neill, C., Lambert, A., Linnell, R., and Warr-Wood, J. (1976) *Drama Guidelines*. London: Heinemann
O'Neill, C. and Lambert, A. (1982) *Drama Structures*. London: Hutchinson
Parsons, B. (1991) Story-making and drama for children 5–8. In S. Wright (Ed.) *The Arts in Early Childhood*. Sydney: Prentice Hall
Pena, S., French, J., and Holmes, R. (1987) A look at superheroes: some issues and guidelines. *Day Care and Early Education*. 15(1), 10–14
Pharo, J. (1992) Assignment submitted to the Institute of Early Childhood, Macquarie University, Australia
Rosen, M. (1982) Becoming our experts. cited in J. Neelands (1984) *Making Sense of Drama*. London: Heinemann
Schaffner, M., Parsons, B., Little, G. and Felton, H. (1984) *Drama, Language and Learning*. NADIE Papers No. 1. Hobart: National Association for Drama in Education

Simons, J. (1991) Concept development and drama: scaffolding the learning. in J. Hughes (ed.) *Drama in Education: the State of the Art. Sydney*: Educational Drama Association of New South Wales

Skatowski, J. (1992) Drama on the margins or could life be imitating theatre? *The National Association for Drama in Education J. (Australia)*. **16**(4) 18-25

Stentiford, L. (1985) *Use of Theatre Form Toward the Education of Feeling*. Leeds: Drama in Metro Leeds, Kemble Press

Vygotsky, L. (1978) Interaction between learning and development. in M. Cole, V. John-Steiner, S. Scribner and E. Souberman (Eds.). *Mind in Society: The Development of Higher Psychological Processes*. Cambridge, Mass.: Harvard University Press

Warren K. (1991) Drama for young children. in J. Hughes (Ed.). *Drama in Education: The State of the Art*. Sydney: Educational Drama Association of NSW

Warren, K. (1992) *Hooked on Drama: The Theory and Practice of Drama in Early Childhood*. Sydney: Institute of Early Childhood: Macquarie University

Wheeler, S. (1991) . . . "from little acorns grow" . . . drama and the under fives. *The Drama Magazine: J. of National Drama*. November: 10, 11

Wilson, G. (1985) *The Psychology of the Performing Arts*. London: Croom Helm

Imagination in learning: learning to imagine

MARGARET H. WHITE

Institute of Early Childhood, Macquarie University

The role of the arts in the development of imagination in early childhood is linked with children's need to explore and learn about their world. Learning to imagine is a crucial step in symbol-making in early childhood. Decentration skills are hypothesised as the link between fantasy or pretense play activities and development in areas such as communication, co-operation, perspective-taking ability, creativity, problem-solving skills and many areas of cognitive development. Children develop their own theories of the world well before starting school and, by being aware of these theories, teachers can build on children's prior learning rather than negating it. Examples of children's symbol-making are used to illustrate the process of making meaning. Aspects of children's learning environments are considered in terms of how effectively they facilitate children's exploration and the development of imagination.

Key words: imagination, decentration, the arts, symbol-making, apprenticeship, childhood

Educational "forecasting" — judging what children need to equip them for the future — has been a preoccupation of educators for many generations. The following quotation, while rather quaint from current perspectives, illustrates this and raises some interesting questions about the place of the arts in education:

Much that is now done in schools is of little importance in the after-life of the child. But if at school a child has been taught to hold his part in a madrigal, to play an instrument in an orchestra, to use a chisel or pencil, paintbrush or modelling tool, to act, to hear, to feel, he will have gained something of infinite worth, something that will enable him to resist the rush and standardization and futile amusements of the modern world, something that will remain when much that is now given so much importance is consigned to the limbo of forgotten and useless things.
F.C. Happold (British Headmaster, 1937)
cited in Cunningham (1939: 378)

Happold seems to suggest that there is some particular experience of "infinite worth" in the arts which will assist in resisting change. However, the statement also raises wider issues about attitudes to change and the relationship between school and society. This headmaster sees the children's experiences in school as separable from their interactions with the outside world, and the school's role as separable from their interactions with the outside world, and the school's role as creating a buffer against the implied vulgarity of that world.

Such attitudes were not uncommon in the 1930's and they had an obvious influence on the role of the arts in education. The arts were often seen as accomplishments, an added extra, the experience of which would encourage refinement and possibly enhance social status, paticularly for girls.

As interest in aspects of development such as perspective-taking, (Flavell, Botkin, Fry, (Jr), Wright and Jarvis, 1968) and the use of symbols (Piaget 1951) has increased, the place of the arts in education has gradually been reassessed. The links between cognition, symbolic functioning and the arts has been the focus of extensive research, such as that of Project Zero founded at Harvard by Nelson Goodman in 1967. Consequent to these studies, it is now widely accepted that children transform their experiences of the world in order to express and interpret them. Images of significance are transformed by the very act of committing them to paper as children paint and draw. In a similar way, the ability to imagine different outcomes or perspectives enables children to deal constructively in finding solutions to problems. This understanding about children's development is in direct contrast to Happold's statement and allows the conceptualisation of a broader role for education, that of involving all children in the excitement and imaginative processes that lead them to explore their world.

DIVERGENT THINKING AND PLAY

Connections between imagination and learning are evident to the observer of early child development. The key factor is play. Play is often appreciated by adults as fundamental to early childhood, yet is rarely recognised in terms of the significance it has in overall development. When young children use a broom or a stick as a horse, they are under no illusions about it's real function, yet, for the purposes of their play, they are able to see it as a horse in addition to being a broom or a stick.

In social play when children take on another role they are also able to retain their awareness of themselves as a child at the same time as taking on a role, "being mother" or "doctor", or "cat". Through participation in such role play children acquire ways of making inferences about other people's thinking and roles and seeing actions from another person's perspective as illustrated in the following example from a case study of Emily aged five:

After a thorough search of the house one day, Emily was finally found, laughing, under the dining table. A few minutes later, assessing the impact of her actions she said, "Next time, when you are looking for me you'll think to yourself, 'I won't look under there because she was there last time' won't you?! (White, 1985: 16)

Fantasy or pretense play activities such as these have been hypothesized as contributing to many aspects of development. The following exchange between two four year olds illustrates this:

Sophie: You're the doctor and I'm the Mum.
David: OK, (puts on a jacket). Now let's have our tea.
Sophie: You don't say that, you say, is that the sick baby, get it?

There is evidence in this exchange of the use of communication, perspective-taking, social problem-solving, meta-linguistic awareness, role definition and some degree of co-operation!

This hypothesis is based on Piaget's (1970: 109) explanation of the development of decentration skills or the ability to consider multiple aspects of situations or things simultaneously. These skills are at least partially responsible for the emergence of the aspects of development mentioned above as well as of dramatic play. Decentration is seen to be the basis not only for the abilities to communicate and take the perspective of others into account, but also for the ability to consider simultaneously the classificatory relationship between parts and the whole.

While Piaget focussed on this area of cognitive development largely in isolation from social or other environmental influences, Vygotsky (1987) pointed to the influence of the social context in shaping the child's point of view. Gardner (1992: 99) observes that ". . . social context provides the setting in which children learn . . . to give public form to their mental representations in service of communication with others." Clearly, play facilitates children's construction of their world through the opportunities it provides to try out different roles and to engage in interactive situations in which children experience responses to their ideas and actions.

EDUCATORS WORKING WITH DECENTRATION

What impact could this understanding have on the way in which adults work with children? The illustration in Figure 1, "Mrs Sideby and Sarah", is a useful example. In a school where children are encouraged to maintain cross-age friendships, two older girls dressed up and appeared in the Kindergarten room where they introduced themselves as "Mrs Sideby and her daughter Sarah" and said "We've come to see if this would be a good school for Sarah". "Entering into the spirit of the 'visit' the teacher answered many questions and encouraged the children to show the 'visitors' around. Finally "Mrs Sideby and Sarah" left after giving their considered view of the school and saying that they were visiting lots of schools but they thought they would like to come back for another visit here.

A few minutes after they left the older girls reappeared without their costumes and casually asked if there had been any visitors around lately. The younger children earnestly told them about Mrs Sideby and Sarah. Afke, four years of age, joined in with a detailed description of their appearance and one of the older girls said "Can you do me a painting of how they looked?" Afke eagerly went and painted the first of many paintings of the "visitors". After the success of their first visit, the older girls continued to make further visits, usually joined by a few other

Figure 1 "Mrs Sideby and Sarah".

older children keen to join in the play. Afke painted her response to each visit and gradually started to suspend her belief that the characters were "real". Finally she persuaded the older girls to take her on as the younger sister of Sarah!

Afke's participation in these episodes raises some interesting questions. Was her ability to decenter influenced on these occasions by her strong desire to participate in the play with the older girls? Did she deliberately suspend her belief that "Mrs Sideby and Sarah" were older girls dressed up in order to participate by taking the role of audience which she perceived was expected of her? An episode such as this can give teachers many insights into the perspective-taking ability of children. By facilitating such interchanges, teachers can enhance children's participation in dramatic play as well as their experiences in considering social situations from different perspectives.

INTUITIVE UNDERSTANDING

Children's comments often indicate the way they are making sense of their world. The following example illustrates this: three children were sitting in a sandpit surrounded by pools of water enclosing hills of sand. Caleb commented "I'm making the Water-Sculpture Centre". The teacher, puzzled by this, asked for more details. Suddenly she put together the relevant facts. Across the road from the school was a Horticulture School which the children visited often. In the gardens was a huge lake with fountains. The children had also been making clay "sculptures" recently. These experiences had been combined into a new understanding. It appears quite an obvious connection to combine sculpture, fountains and water, yet how many comments such as Caleb's are passed over daily by teachers without recognition of the significance of the connections which children are making for themselves?

Children's Theories of the World

In recent years Gardner (1991) has focussed on the development of four-and-five-year-olds, looking at what he calls "the emergence of their intuitive understanding". Above all, children of this age are exploring and experimenting with their world and starting to relate that experience to what they gradually understand to be the adult world. Gardner (1991: 84) identifies what he calls ". . . senses of three overlapping realms" which children have developed by this age and which he explains as follows:

In the world of physical objects, they have developed a theory of matter; in the world of living organisms, they have developed a theory of life; and in the world of human beings, they have a theory of the mind that incorporates a theory of the self.

These "theories" both inform and are informed by the experimenting and exploration which young children pursue, whatever their circumstances. They allow children to make sense of the world in a way that is appropriate for them and yet be flexible enough to encompass further experiences. An example of a child making sense of his world which incorporates several aspects of these "theories" follows in Christian's story:

Christian, aged 5 years was the youngest child in a much older family. He had many people who were interested to explore ideas with him, to ask and answer questions. At the time of this anecdote he was in a group of five year olds from diverse backgrounds. He entered group as a rather anxious child, separation from his mother was uneasy, and his experience with many adults meant that it was quite difficult for him to be a member of a peer group, to listen to other opinions and take the perspective of others.

One child in particular, Michael, was very confronting for Christian. He was seen by the other children as "cool", that is, he had a wry sense of humour, was mischevious at times and was very adventurous. Christian, in contrast, was very concerned about right and wrong, was physically cautious, and more involved with creating an accurate view of the world than inverting facts to create humour. Interestingly, Michael came from a background where he too had alot of adult attention as he was an only child in an a very close family. His grandparents were Jewish and it was clear that Michael had a close relationship with his grandmother who told him many stories. This often led to him raising complex questions at school such as "Did the Jews kill Jesus?", "Was Noah's Ark in Ancient Times?". Another parallel here was that Christian attended an Anglican Sunday School fairly regularly.

The story (as seen in Figures 2-4) was drawn by Christian towards the end of the year, and an adult acted as scribe for him. In essence, this overview of the life of Christ, expressed in four drawings includes the most graphic moments, explained with apparent simplicity.

The drawings are simple outline shapes with emphasis on the communication of detail, for example, the nails and the relative size and number of people. (The representation of people was a fairly recently-developed skill.). In his use of the Southern Cross (a constellation of stars in the Southern Hemisphere), Christian

The baby got laid in the manger and the King wanted to put him on the Southern Cross.

Figure 2.1 Christian's Story.

> They hammerd him onto the Southern Cross. You can see the nails.

Figure 2.2 Christian's Story.

is drawing together details of his general knowledge in a way that satisfies his need to describe a powerful image and which makes sense for him.

The facts as we understand them are retold making an explicable story, ("They all thought that he was so bad that he didn't know about God . . .") out of information which, for a five-year-old, is largely inexplicable.

As Christian drew he talked about the characters in a way that suggested that he was in the process of making meaning of the stories as he was drawing. Finally, when the book was finished, Christian ran up to Michael to show him the story.

Michael's response: "It wasn't the Southern Cross! That's in the sky!"
Christian: "Well Jesus is in the sky, he's everywhere."
Michael: "Well I know, it WASN'T the Southern Cross"
Christian: "Well I can have it the Southern Cross if I want to, it's MY book!"

> They all thought that he was so bad that he didn't know about God. And so they put him on the Southern Cross.

Figure 2.3 Christian's Story.

Outside the drama of the story another agenda was being played, that of the validity to Christian, of his own representations and meaning-making, and his increasing confidence to assert his independence while also recognising that Michael could hold a different view without this threatening his own view.

Returning to Gardner's view of children's theories of the world, what does Christian's story tell us about his theories? How should a teacher respond to such an episode? In this instance, Christian's theory involving God, the stars and Jesus on the Cross, suggests that he is taking a stance towards the world and creating

> There he is on the Southern Cross and he's dead.

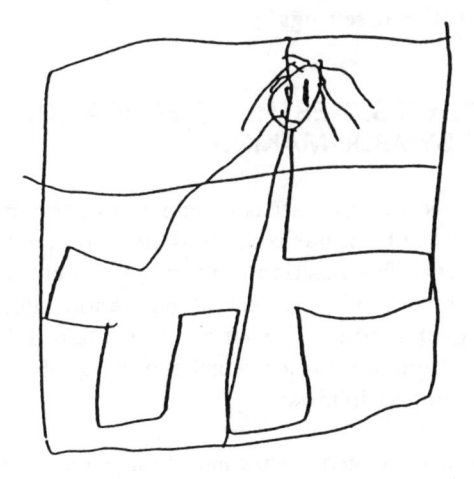

Figure 2.4 Christian's Story.

his own theory which combines some powerful images. The fact that this theory does not coincide with that held by those around him raises some significant questions for educators. Should the teacher intervene in the situation between Michael and Christian? Should Christian be "taught" factual information about the solar system and the Bible story? Should he be left with his intuitive understanding until he further develops his own theories? Christian's clarity about himself as a separate entity is evident, suggesting that his theory of self is serving him well as he negotiates the world of school. To attempt an answer the earlier questions there are several other aspects of learning which need to be explored.

INTUITIVE LEARNING AND SCHOLASTIC LEARNING

So far, the examples used have shown children engaged in learning by making sense of their world. All these examples have been collected from young children. What happens when these children enter the world of school? How is this intuitive learning harnessed within a school environment?

> Somehow the natural, universal, or intuitive learning that takes place in one's home or immediate surroundings during the first years of life seems of an entirely different order from school learning that is now required throughout the literate world. (Gardner, 1991: 2)

Gardner (1991) contrasts intuitive learning with scholastic learning. He suggests that even when schools are seen to be successful, they fail to achieve their goals. He also documents research with honours-level college students who are unable to solve basic problems and questions encountered in a form slightly different from that on which they have been formally instructed and tested. Clearly there is a large gap between early childhood experiences and later modes of learning. It seems that Happold's view of school and society being separable is still pervasive in many Western educational settings.

EDUCATING THE SENSES: AESTHETIC EDUCATION AND THE DEVELOPMENT OF SYMBOL-MAKING

The term "aesthetic" has, in some areas of education, become a concept to be avoided. In recent years the term has come to denote to many people an esoteric and elitist view of the arts. This reaction to previous use of the term has resulted in temporary confusion in a vital aspect of education. Peter Abbs (1989: 4) addresses the meaning of aesthetic by citing The Oxford English Dictionary derivation of aesthetic from the Greek word meaning 'through the senses' to clarify his use of the word as follows:

"The aesthetic, far from being 'esoteric' is the most basic mode of human response. The tiny child, the new-born baby, begins to mediate its world aesthetically: through touch, taste, smell, sound, feel."

The way in which children respond to the perceptions of the senses is clearly the most effective starting-point for education. The development in early infancy from dependence on direct bodily expression to the use of more symbolic expressions (eg crying to asking, grabbing to pointing) and later from spontaneous responses to more sociocultural forms of representation (eg subjective portrayals to realism) is fundamental to our understanding of the development of creativity and imagination in human functioning.

As cited earlier, children are negotiating between the real world and the imagined one. In each child's development, the point at which expression of experiencing (using all the senses) takes on a symbolic form, is possibly one of the most crucial in terms of education. Educators need to be aware that symbolization occurs at both a private and a shared level, and children need to achieve a balance between these two aspects. Transforming and elaborating upon experiences through symbol-making whether it be in music, drawing, sculpting, dancing, writing or another expressive form, is one of children's major ways of learning about their world.

HOW CAN ADULTS ENGAGE CHILDREN WITH THEIR LEARNING?

Time to play (not only in the early childhood years), an environment to explore and investigate, materials which are basic to exploration and support from adults who observe, respond and encourage reflection are four basic requirements which need attention if children are to have the possibility of developing an open and enquiring mind and engaging in fruitful and satisfying forms of expression.

Time
The time which was available to today's adults as children, to explore and reflect in a familiar environment, is often taken up for today's children with television, homework and other commitments. While one would certainly not advocate a Luddite-view of restricting children's experience of their world, it takes initiative on the part of adults to ensure that children have unstructured time in which to play hence to construct their own world.

Environment
Children are resourceful and, if left to their own resources, find many things to explore in environments which adults may view as limited. Physical environments which encourage exploration generally have tactile qualities, plants and contrasting surfaces, things to handle, space to construct, and preferably earth, sand and water.

Materials
Leading on from elemental materials, the availability of basic materials for symbol-making need not involve large expense. Clay, paint, paper, pencils, and adhesive, form the basis for a collection of materials which children can add to as their needs develop.

Support
By far the most significant of these requirements is the need for support. The adult to observe, to share the experience, to respond to the symbol-making and to reflect upon events, enhances the insights which each child gains from their exploration. Of course, much of the time to explore is with peers, siblings or alone. The adult can become a reference-point, and as children grow older they are able to seek the support they need from a variety of people.

A Reappraisal Of Two Familiar Modes of Learning

There are two ways of learning which are being increasingly considered with interest by those people who believe that there is urgent need for a reappraisal of the way in which genuine understanding is developed.

The learning environment of museums
As museums have developed more interactive ways of functioning, so people are becoming aware of the rich potential they hold for engaging children with a wide

range of experiences; in the arts, sciences, history, in fact almost any area of human experience. The open-endedness of museums enables children to ask questions and explore ideas in an environment which is full of potential for discovery and which feeds the imagination of both children and adults.

Apprenticeship as a model

Earlier we considered the circumstances that children encounter when they approach scholastic learning. Open enquiry which has been so much part of early childhood, and the symbol-making which enables children to represent their world and to develop meaning, are frequently at odds with the agenda of the school.

Over the past decade some attention has been focused again on the apprenticeship model which was previously the method by which tradespeople were trained by more experienced "teachers". As researchers have looked more closely at the interactions and learning patterns which occur in this working relationship, they have realised that many of the most valuable elements of education are embodied within it. And most significantly, this learning is contextualised. That is, the reasons for learning are evident in the situation in which the learning takes place.

Mention was made earlier of Vygotsky's work in relation to the influences the social context has in shaping the child's point of view. Contemporary research by Rogoff (1990) draws on the work of Vygotsky and his theory of the zone of proximal development. Rogoff (1990: 141) outlines the way in which social interaction facilitates cognitive development. As children work closely with a person with more skill (this may be another child or an adult), they are able to participate in tasks which would be beyond them if they worked independently. The emphasis in this situation is on sharing skills and collaborating rather than the traditional adult-child instructional model.

Recalling the questions that were posed in relation to Christian's story, it becomes apparent that working in a context which encourages a child to explore, to test out theories, and experience the stimulus of exchanging ideas in a collaborative situation, more effectively serves the child's needs than a didactic or prescriptive approach which would be likely to both frustrate the enthusiastic search for knowledge and limit an imaginative approach to exploring the world.

How then, can adults engage children with their learning? The implications of Rogoff's research are for teachers to recognize that in any context their interactions with a child may be a potent influence in shaping the child's point of view. By being aware of the significance of the connections which children are making, how they are theorising about the world and the role imagination plays in their learning, teachers can collaborate with children to open up the possibilities for more responsive interaction, thereby building on and enhancing children's intuitive learning.

References

Abbs, P. (1989) *The Symbolic Order*. London: Falmer Press
Cunningham, K.S. (Ed.). (1938) *Education for Complete Living*. Melbourne: Australian Council for Educational Research
Flavell, J.H., Botkin, P.T., Fry, C.L. (Jr.), Wright, J.W., and Jarvis, P.E. (1968) *The Development of Role-Taking and Communication Skills in Children*. New York: Wiley
Gardner, H. (1991) *The Unschooled Mind: How children think and how schools should teach*. USA: Basic Books
Gardner, H. (1992) The Cognitive Revolution: Consequences for the Understanding and Education of the Child as an Artist. In B. Reimer, & R.A. Smith, *The Arts, Education, and Aesthetic Knowing*. Chicago: National Society for the Study of Education
Piaget, J. (1951). *Play, Dreams and Imitation in Childhood*. New York: W.W. Norton
Piaget, J. (1970) In P.H. Mussen (Ed.) (1983), *Handbook of Child Psychology* (Vol. 1). New York: Wiley
Rogoff, B. (1990) *Apprenticeship in Thinking*. Oxford: Oxford University Press
Vygotsky, L. (1987) *Thought and Language*, edited by Alex Kozulin. Cambridge: MIT Press
White, M.H. (1985) *Three Case Studies of Children Involved in the Performing Arts*. (Unpublished paper). University of Sydney

The role of the early childhood advisor in children's television production

HELEN MARTIN

Australian Broadcasting Commission Television, Sydney

The challenge for the Early Childhood Adviser to *Play School* is to make the theory and philosophy of early childhood accessible, relevant and clearly articulated in the production of children's television. This article explores the means by which this is achieved in the Australian production of *Play School*.

Particular attention is given to perceptual considerations for setting, staging, materials used, selection of camera shots, the use of language and visual and verbal matching in scripting and recording. Special features of *Play School* include the clarification of reality and fantasy through visual and verbal presentation, as well as the child-presenter interaction.

Key words: Children and television, early childhood adviser, television production, values, child-presenter interaction.

"Play School number 126, Wednesday . . . stand by for recording!"

At the Australian Broadcasting Commission (ABC), in studio 22, the production of another children's television program is under-way. By the end of the day a thirty-minute episode of *Play School* will be complete, safely stored on video, and ready for transmission across Australia.

A few weeks later at 9:30 a.m. or 4:00 p.m. the program will go to air with the words — "Open wide come inside, it's *Play School*. These last lines of the well known title song act as a signal for thousands of young children that it is time to tune in; "Their"' program is ready to begin. According to *Play School* viewing reports, which record responses of children 0-5 years of age who have watched the program (and also record comments of the adult viewing-audience), many carers settle children to watch the program, secure in the knowledge that it does cater specifically for a child audience in the 2-5 year age-range.

HOW DOES PLAYSCHOOL CATER FOR THE VERY YOUNG TELEVISION VIEWER?

Studies of children and television fall into two main strands. The earlier, "reactive" theory, which focused on the formal features of television programs such as perceptual salience and television's effect on children's auditory and visual attention, maximised the effect of television on the passive viewer. The later, theoretical strand saw the child as an active, schema-driven viewer which, in turn, led to greater focus on individual characteristics and the potential contribution of developmental theories to an understanding of the processes of children's television viewing. Anderson & Lorch (1983) saw the content and form of a television program as just one part of a three way interaction as follows:

Rather than being a reaction to the screen, we have come to see television viewing as an active cognitive transaction between the young viewer, the television and the viewing environment.

Here the focus was on the individual characteristics of the "active viewer", with the child's development, ability, interest and experience being seen as mediators of television effects.

Play School, in terms of format, style of presentation and content reflects its "developmental" bias. Noble (1992) supports the premise that the program is firmly based on the concept of the child as an active viewer and aims to encourage both interaction and participation. Accordingly, *Play School* offers a personal, process-orientated rather than goal-centred approach. In contrast *Sesame Street* is an example of the latter approach where the learning of letters, numbers, vocabulary and social skills underpins the program. This is reflected in the use of formal features to attract attention such as the advertising mode of editing, which uses short, snappy, persuasive segments ("Sesame Street was brought to you today by the letter 'Y' and numbers 3 and 6...."). In contrast, *Play School* chooses a lifepace style of presentation with no specific target stated.

Play School was originally a British Broadcasting Commission (BBC) television program. Over 27 years it has developed a uniquely Australian flavour and individual style, but maintained a commitment to the child-centred approach as used by the BBC. It is no surprise, therefore, that the original BBC *Play School* program reflected the child-centred philosophy of British Primary School Education in the 1970's. An early study by Gwen Dunn (1974) *Television And The Pre School Child* was influential in the development of interest in the effects of television on very young children. Her updated study, (1977) published as a book entitled *The Box In The corner: Television And The Under Fives*, included observations of children and discussion with parents, teachers and production personnel. An initial concern of Dunn's was possibility of incompatibility arising from an essential difference between the world of pre-school television and the world of little children. Everything in the television world is fast-paced and somewhat impersonal, where work consists of tightly scheduled deadlines imposed in order to achieve a specific visual outcome. In marked contrast, the child's world is one of deferment and distraction: It a personal, emotional world without a particular long term aim or goal. While Dunn found qualified support for the view that television could benefit young children (particularly with regard to the development of oracy), she stressed the importance of, and the need to communicate to **production personnel**, the idea that very young children see the world from a special perspective. This aspect of Dunn's work is something of a model for the role of the Early Childhood Adviser to the Australian *Play School* program produced for ABC TV.

WHAT IS THE ROLE OF THE EARLY CHILDHOOD ADVISER IN THE TELEVISION PROGRAM PLAY SCHOOL?

To the casual observer, *Play School* often appears to be a straight-forward, spontaneous program. A couple of friendly-looking people chat to children, make a variety of craft items, sing action songs and move around, dressing-up or imitating animals with much vigour and enthusiasm. However, the "casual air" is deceptive, for the completed program is the culmination of months of planning and intensive interaction (within a team of out-liners, producers, designers, technical crew and an Early Childhood Adviser). Nevertheless, the production team would be pleased and relieved to hear that the program does achieve a look of spontaneity, informality and creativity, because this is precisely what is intended.

In this *Play School* team, the role of the Early Childhood Adviser is a unique one in that it includes both early childhood and television production issues, requires a sound knowledge of both fields, and both intuitive and firmly-grounded decision-making. Within the ABC itself, the role is an anomaly, for it does not fit into any pre-existing staff category, but its existence is a measure of the National Broadcaster's commitment to quality programming for young children.

To the often-asked question: "What is an Early Childhood Adviser in television production?" the simplistic answer might be: "A resident four-year-old" because the main task of the adviser is to present a view-point and the likely responses of a pre-school child, in order to brief members of the production team. Naturally this entails far more than a child-like response to suggested material! The Adviser needs to communicate as clearly as possible the very young child's "state of being" — that is the child's general developmental level, significant competencies and dominant interests. Such communicated knowledge then allows personnel involved in children's television, to make judgements about the appropriateness of selected content, materials, and settings, as well as choices about the technical elements in the presentation of ideas.

The role of the Early Childhood Adviser also involves considerable liaison responsibilities such as keeping abreast of current early childhood theory and significant new studies which might influence attitudes and the approach to specific curriculum areas such as music, or general issues such as multiculturalism. It is necessary to keep in close contact with practitioners working in the field, to observe a range of services and settings, to discuss innovative ideas and practices, and specifically, to observe children's reactions to each new *Play School* program. The real challenge then, is to communicate this knowledge effectively to production personnel in such a way that the considerations are reflected positively and practically through the television medium. Hence, both content and technical considerations are involved in clearly communicating to adults, the 'essence' of being a preschool child.

The underlying philosophy of the *Play School* program provides an obvious point at which to start with new producers, designers and actors. However, philosophy can be difficult to grasp. How does one explain a four-year-old's perspective (even if it could be neatly packaged) to a new producer whose primary concern to-date has been with the production of an exciting, "high-tech" feature program for young adult television viewers? Such a producer might have used the latest techniques of camera and chroma-key to create exciting rapidly changing visual images. These might be stimulating in pace, heightened emotionally by powerful music and by mixing reality and fantasy in eye-catching transformations (as for example, when the vision switcher "magically" dissolves from the head of an angry man into a screen-filling image of a snarling wolf). Alternatively, a new producer may come to the program with a background in high school teaching, a strong interest in a specific curriculum area and a zeal to impart this knowledge through the medium of television, whereas the new designer may have great talent for creating vast, modern, surrealist sets, full of sharp angles and distorted objects. Meshing these people with such different ideas, priorities and talents into a children's television production team requires specific input from the Early Childhood Adviser and tactful intervention in leading towards a particular, planned approach. The process of building an appreciation of young children's competencies also takes time, but is essential for sympathetic work, particularly since the focus of the program is that of the relationship established between the viewing child and the television presenter (which will be discussed later in this article).

HOW ARE FUNDAMENTAL CONCEPTS OF EARLY CHILDHOOD COMMUNICATED TO PRODUCTION PERSONNEL?

Visits to child care centres and observation of children's play as well as group and home-based viewing of programs, provide a practical basis for reference and discussion for the Early Childhood Adviser. In order to avoid a didactic, overly-informative approach to programs, early emphasis is placed on *Play School* as a program for young children's entertainment which offers opportunities for learning. *Play School* is not a formal teaching program, although it is felt children do learn through participation. Perhaps the word "School" in the *Play School* title confuses the issue somewhat for it might suggest that the program formally "teaches" children. The philosophy is based, however, on the idea that young children learn in a holistic way through care and play, that is, in interactive experience with their world. This is in accordance with the majority of theorists, training institutions and early childhood centres in Australia. The belief that play is a vital part of a young child's development is affirmed in the Australian Early Childhood Association Code of Ethics (1989, 1991). The challenge for the Early Childhood Adviser is to make this theory and philosophy accessible, relevant and clearly articulated in the production of children's television.

A simple analogy can often communicate effectively a complicated idea. By referring to "learning holistically", one might suggest that children are not seen as "patchwork rugs", divided up into neat little segments — the maths bit, the creative bit, the verbal bit, the physical bit and so on ... All these aspects are developing simultaneously as the child actively seeks interaction with material and people in her world, (although she may focus selectively on one area at a time). Through experiencing, the child is learning about herself as an individual and as a social being.

The Adviser must then find ways of exemplifying this for the busy producer or designer who may have little or limited experience with young children. On-the-spot observation can be supported with comments (from the Adviser) on the possible discoveries taking place as a child engages in a play activity. For instance, if a child is undressing and washing a doll's dress the following discoveries may be taking place:

- She might be exercising fine motor muscles by squeezing and rubbing the material;
- She might be learning about the nature of water (wet and warm) and the sensory qualities of soap (slippery and slimy) or
- The fact that soap makes bubbles, that it gets dirt out and that it tastes yuk!

On the other hand she might be making a mathematical discovery that size and shape are significant, that the small shirt will not fit over the doll's large head and the doll must be bathed in the clothes. That is discovery learning for a child! Then again, the child might be involved in a symbolic replay of her own social experience with her care giver, playing out her fears, or trying out another authority role. [Children often talk to themselves and toys — assigning roles: "There now, just shut your eyes this won't hurt ... don't be a silly girl ..." "Now don't cry!"]. Perhaps an experimental plunge of the baby doll's head under water might release a few negative feelings triggered off by a new baby in the house, a crisis which the child has not quite come to terms with at home. Therefore, bathing the doll and washing clothes might be an important step in the child's emotional development or the observer might be overstating the significance of the event for the child. Nevertheless, discussion arises naturally from such observed examples.

The next step is not so difficult. Busy producers have little time to fully study child development theory such as the Piagetian concept of assimilation and accommodation. However, because *Play School* takes account of the pre-operational stage of development, the Adviser needs to provide a simplified yet still practical way of clarifying these concepts. For instance, one might suggest that with so much to learn, the child has to focus and select what is relevant to her right now in order to develop new concepts. This putting together of the pieces of the puzzle in a personal way, as *she* sees fit, is very important to the child. Most importantly, the mental "picture" created by the child at this point will probably be a very different "picture" from the one that an adult has of the same situation. Again, a specific practical example might serve to illustrate this:

A young teacher having involved her pre-school group in an experimental learning situation about dogs felt satisfied that the concept had been explored, vocabulary extended and plenty of time given for hands-on experience. On a walk with children later in the week she saw a large dog which was covered with tightly curled hair. "Look at that woolly dog" she remarked pointing to the unusually furry animal. One small boy looked at the dog for a long moment, then at his new jumper, then back at the dog. Finally he asked very seriously, "Who knitted that dog Miss B?"

From his point of view, with his accumulated pieces of knowledge, that was a very logical question. The kind of ground-work illustrated by using observation examples and discussion of these issues, assists a new production-unit member in understanding the *Play School* philosophy. If the program purports not to teach formally, why is this knowledge of play and learning about play important? It is, after all, a television program, which means that children are not sharing the same physical space and so cannot have the same first-hand experience as children in real-life circumstances. These are valid points. However, the role of children's play does have a pivotal effect on the program in consideration of both content and presentation. As a consequence, *Play School* is said to know it's audience, it's "level" and way of learning very well.

Play School Presentation of Ideas

Play School takes the young child's approach to play as a model for presenting different activities, not exactly by playing **as children**, but rather in the philosophical approach used. The program works in a natural life-time and place, emphasising the reality of situations. There is integration of themes and a balance of activities. Each day of a week of themes explores different concepts, and ideas related to the theme are explored. Each *Play School* day is based loosely on five areas: art and craft, the social world, the natural world, imaginative play and scientific inquiry.

If one was working on a cat theme for instance, a paper-plate cat might be constructed as an art and craft component and "Hey Diddle Diddle" recited and sung for language. Music might involve listening to instruments that create "Yeowly" sounds. A problem solving situation might be set up and finally the presenter may climb on a block to put the toy cat, Diddle, up over the moon as a dramatisation effect. A real cat and kittens may be the focus for a natural world segment and afford the presenter an opportunity to discuss the soft padded paws of a cat, and then move like a cat in an imaginative cat and mouse game. Perhaps a few scientific facts on the cat's whiskers may also be presented as part of the theme.

Woven into this theme are further songs, stories and poems that relate in a variety of ways to the content of the segments. From a specific focus on cat sounds, a musical segment might be developed, exploring the sounds made by a selection of cross-cultural, stringed instruments, followed by the singing of a well known Greek musical participation song. This may extend into the making of a simple stringed instrument out of a box, by which time a link back to the theme of "cats" is possible via the nonsense story/song "The Owl and the Pussy Cat" which could then be dramatised. A sub-theme for the week might be "caring". Activities which explore this concept in a crosscultural way, would be woven through the day in a similar manner. So, throughout the week, themes for focus, diversions to delight, sub-themes to extend and as much material as possible that reflects the modern multicultural society in which we live, are integrated into the program.

PRACTICAL IMPLICATIONS OF THE EARLY CHILDHOOD PHILOSOPHY FOR PRODUCTION.

Once the philosophical basis for *Play School* has been established, it is far easier to discuss specific, practical details and considerations with production members. However, with all areas of the production process affected by the underlying philosophy, it is necessary to select the most relevant for discussion. Perhaps initial consideration of the "look" of the program provides a useful starting point. The set is made up of standard pieces of equipment including functional items such as cupboards, shelves, tables, stools, pinning boards and blocks, whereas special feature items such as the story chair and the windows are selected, arranged and "dressed" in a style that should reflect the designer's specific knowledge as well as the content of the program. The set and the dressing give a powerful message and it is important to clarify what the program tries to communicate through this. *Play School* ideally functions as a bridging place somewhere between the warm, familiar comfort of a home environment and the more multi-purpose, group-efficient environment of a kindergarten or daycare centre. Jim Greenman (1991), stressed the need for the emotional, social and cognitive needs of the child to be met as well as the more obvious physical needs taken into account when planning buildings and equipment for early childhood centres. He emphasised that child-friendly spaces were part of good design in such centres. *Play School* tries to project a friendly, colourful, secure, yet flexible atmosphere; a known, comfortable place where interesting, inventive, serious and funny things can happen.

One aspect of the Adviser's role on *Play School* is to negotiate for balance between the visual ideals of line and design, and the messy, creative, "do-it-yourself" pre-school world. This applies to graphics, sets and dressing. Strong modules that emphasise towering angularity, and a monochromatic colour scheme which may intrigue an adult, can be alienating and overwhelming for a small child. On the other hand over-cluttered, highly-coloured and patterned sets can distract the eye, demand attention that draws focus away from the foreground person or object, and set up a confusion of figure and ground. The presenter may not be seen as the directly-important focus, and objects that are being "studied" (unless on a close-up camera shot) may be hard to distinguish from the overly-busy background. Thus, the issues of camera shots and scripting must be considered in relation to the pre-school child's perspective and how it affects camera shots selected in scripting directions for the studio.

Dunn's (1977) study recognised the young child's "special perspective".

Whereas adults take for granted their ability to perceive objects accurately, a small child may not recognise all items with ease. Young children often experience difficulty with part-whole spatial concepts (Donaldson, 1978). If part of an object is shown on screen without some context, or if the camera angle is extreme (thus giving a distorted and unfamiliar perspective), it can be confusing and unrecognisable to a three year old. Indeed some images on screen also can be confusing to adults. Consider this example:

Imagine a close-up shot of a dripping tap, taken from above, appears suddenly on the screen without a contextual reference of any kind. A fast zoom down to a big close-up fills the screen with the object magnified several times beyond the object's real size. Part of a hand then intrudes and rotates the tap handle then the whole image dissolves into a soft haze of light as drop of water splashes into a pool.

It is abstract, it can be beautiful, but is it clear to a child of 3 or 4 years?

To "decode" this object, the adult must work much in the manner of a young child, putting together the puzzling pieces and fitting these new images together with previously absorbed knowledge, in order to clarify and contextualize. Gardner (1983) and associates differ from Piaget in suggesting that what differentiates the child from the adult in this situation is not so much the process as the fact that the adult's frame of reference is so much broader. The adult has built a store of knowledge and experience about a particular object and its function, has seen objects from differing perspectives and recognised through practice and observation, the part-whole relationship of an object. This knowledge base, and an understanding of cause and effect combined with a media "vocabulary", enables the adult to recognise that it is the technology of television (that is the studio camera and vision mixer) that produces the effect of one image transforming into another.

A delightful study by Rheta De Vries (1967) in which a cat's face was covered with a rabbit mask, found support for the theory that three to six-year-olds struggle with the concept of cause and effect, leading to a difficulty in distinguishing reality from their own perceived view. One might imply from this that very young children have difficulty in distinguishing between reality and fantasy. The visual impact of the rabbit mask persuaded the children that the cat *was* a rabbit, even when the mask was put on the cat in front of the children. The important point for television programming is that it strongly supports the premise that the visual image presented to (or seen by) three to five-year-old children dominates their perception of it. It suggests that their ability to de-structure multifaceted images developed by sophisticated camera work is limited. The ABC viewing reports indicate that the effect of highly-stylised or exaggerated presentations on small children can range from mild bemusement to high levels of frustration and concern if the material is consistently too difficult or if a child's security is threatened. *Play School* viewing reports (1990) recorded that when the actor Philip Quast donned a costume & whiskers for a game, a three-year-old kept asking whether Philip would be coming back?. Following this report, a decision was made not to use the technique of chroma-key in a later program, thereby transporting the presenter into a model world of dinosaurs, particularly since the program tried to reflect the idea that dinosaurs were extinct.

This is not to say that innovative visual techniques of production and camera work are inappropriate. They can be stimulating, challenging and delightful. However, since *Play School* sets out to clarify distinctions between reality and fantasy, the commitment is to simple camera work, shot from the perspective of the watching child, unless a switch to the imaginative realm is indicated. In this case clear signals, both verbal and physical, are given. For example, "We'll see some camera tricks" — a look to the windows followed by a dissolve through to a film shot outside the *Play School* environment, may give children "cues" as to what comes next and may help build media literacy. The presenters on *Play School* cannot transform themselves into magical beings and suddenly fly in the air, but they might dress up and make a box rocket in imaginative play. Similarly, the toys on *Play School* have no "life" of their own other than that endowed by the presenters. The emphasis in the program is on the use of imagination to create belief, followed by a reassuring return to a realistic, recognisable world for the young viewer.

USE OF LANGUAGE ON PLAY SCHOOL

Dunn's (1977) study stressed the need for producers of pre-school programs to be aware that giving children an accurate view of their world was important for the development of language. It was critical that they were able to link the right word to an object that was as readily identifiable as possible, so that half-known vocabulary could be strongly attached. Kendall (1978) the then Executive Producer of *Play School*, commented that long flows of words are difficult for a four year old. Therefore, compound or complex sentence structures are avoided in scripting, and vocabulary selected is within a young child's range of experience as far as possible. In *Play School* words and the objects to which they refer are shown simultaneously, and the same applies for the use of concepts. This works within an integrated sequence which is carefully scripted and revised.

Language is given a central focus on *Play School*, from the scripting through to its final performance. The Early Childhood Adviser is involved throughout this process. A series of meetings is attended variously by the Executive Producer, a script outliner, the Producer and the Adviser during which all practical elements are explored and selected. The script is then written by the Producer and edited by the Adviser in a word-specific way to ensure that the visual image of the object seen by the viewing child accurately reflects the words spoken over it. Verbal links can be used to prepare the child for the image which follows. The Adviser helps to ensure that the script is written "visually and verbally". Clarity and selection are vital since a wash of words can overwhelm small children and the irrelevance of words used in this way can be counter-productive (Dunn, 1974).

An example of a *Play School* sequence might be useful in illustrating this point.

Suppose that the image to be seen on the screen is that of a horse, and the shot is wide, showing the full-size animal in a paddock, flicking its tail. This gives a contextual reference for the child and it is appropriate to use descriptive vocabulary such as "horse", "paddock", "tail", perhaps even "flicking" and "to and fro" if these are clearly demonstrated. The fact that a horse has "hair on its neck" might be a preparatory comment before the next shot, which shows a closer view of the head, neck and mane. Now the word "mane" is used as the camera zooms in to a close-up, allowing a perfect match of word and image. Of course, there are always "lost" moments, particularly when a presenter has to follow a quickly-moving film clip and is caught two beats behind. However, attention to visual and vocal matching is a general rule in preparation and production.

Noble (1979–80) discusses *Play School*'s approach and comments on the use of associated language and the structuring or scaffolding inherent in the program, thus:

Whether Play School producers are aware of the analogy, Play School remains a classic example of what Vygotsky (1962) calls a chain complex; "a dynamic, consecutive joining of individual links into a single chain, with meaning carried over from one link to the next". In their attempt to construct the total "gestalt" of the program, the linkage between items is in terms of a single common attribute. But whereas the chain complex, according to Vygotsky "does not rise above its elements as does a concept", Play School employs this technique merely to link items. They refer back at every opportune moment to their central theme or concept. It is Vygotsky's point that young children think in complexes not concepts, and accounts *inter alia* for "the peculiar phenomenon that one word may in different situations have different or even opposite meanings as long as there is some associative link between them" (as occurred in ancient languages). (Noble, 1980 p 3)

Play School values and uses words in a variety of ways. Specific vocabulary is used for the clarification of concepts. Attention is also paid to word play and the literary delights of language in more formal segments such as the story. Presenters 'share' the sensory nature of objects through word play — using onomatopoeia, rhyme, and repetition which often develops into musical or dramatic sequences. However, there is a further purpose in such verbal activity — that of maintaining the child-presenter relationship.

FEATURES OF THE CHILD-PRESENTER RELATIONSHIP

The attention to careful scripting and encouragement of a life-paced presentation sets up the opportunity for the watching child to respond actively. Noble (1979–80) sees the interactive relationship between the TV presenter and the child as potentially valuable.

To understand that children think that presenters on television talk just to them, and that they can respond and talk back to the presenter necessarily means that televiewing need not be a passive experience. (Noble, 1979–80, p. 22)

Noble's term for this kind of interaction is "para-social". The underlying assumption is that it does work because the child believes the relationship to be actual and immediate. The format, the scripting and the presentation of the program create an illusion of intimacy and allow time and space for a child to respond. The Adviser works both at the script stage and during rehearsals to monitor this.

LIFE-PACED INTERACTION

All the ideas on *Play School* are presented so that children can watch ... follow ... "He's putting that hat on now" ... react ... "I like that one" ... "Ooh Yuk!" or interact. When the presenter John Hamblin, dressed as Little Bo Peep asks "Do I look lovely?" they shriek with delight "No, you look silly!". Then, later, children can re-create ideas in their own way. In this para-social situation children respond to their adult friends, the presenters, secure in the knowledge that they will remain adults, but ones who understand and enjoy things as children do.

THE ACTOR AS A PLAYSCHOOL PRESENTER

The warm manner and the direct "eye contact" approach to the camera by presenters personalise the questions and invitations put forward in the program so that children do feel that they know the presenters and are known by them. Viewing reports, letters to presenters, and verbal comments made to presenters confirm this: John Waters, approached by a young boy in a supermarket, is told confidently "but you know I'm three, don't you?" Noni Hazlehurst is greeted by a child in the street: "Hello, Noni. Do you want to come to my house today?". Letters arrive every week: "Dear Benita, I drew a picture of you, love Ellie. P.S. My mum is writing this for me." Or "Dear George, I like you when you are funny and do the wobbly walk, From Jonathan." A telling comment came from a child watching a new presenter on television. Despite a vigorous invitation, she sat stoically through a song without participating, then remarked "I don't like him." Another child turned to her and said "You don't know him." As in real life, one has to prove one's worth before being counted as a friend.

Part of the Adviser's job is to help the actor understand and feel comfortable with this unique on-screen relationship with the child. Actors are often vulnerable and find it hard not to put on an "acting mask", since performing directly to camera can be very confronting. One is quite likely to feel foolish in a *Play School* sequence, particularly if the requirement is, for example, to cry and crawl as a baby. Noni Hazlehurst speaks of a commitment to the honesty of the moment, responding in a real way to events as they happen. In order for the program to succeed, the child needs to feel that there is a real person talking to them rather than a television personality giving a performance. The Adviser might arrange visits to early childhood centres for the new presenter who does not have much contact with small children in order to help the actor to identify and believe in the typical interests and responses of young children. Supportive feedback is appreciated (given directly or through the producer) on such aspects as the pace and timing of songs and stories and activities which require question and answer patterns from the viewers. Above all, the Adviser encourages the actor to speak through the camera to one individual child.

A noted feature of learning to relax as a presenter is the ability to make mistakes and to allow oneself to look silly. *Play School* tries to encourage the idea that things can be invented and used in a variety of ways. There is no right way or wrong way to do it (though some ways are definitely more successful than others). For children, the process is more important at this stage than the product. This might explain in part John Hamblin's great popularity as a presenter. He understands a child's feelings of inadequacy very well. He is the one who never quite gets the dance steps right, muddles up the words of a song, or makes the aeroplane with lopsided wings. Affectionately know as "Silly John", he is enormously reassuring to children who can laugh with him and feel that it is all right not to be perfect.

The relationship with presenters is the linchpin of *Play School*. The content, the format, and the stylistic features of the program all relate to the central premise that the very young child interacts in a positive way with that screen presence — the presenter — who chooses to share with the child time, items that reflect her interests, capabilities and concerns and who offers her delight and entertainment.

CONCLUDING COMMENTS

The areas discussed in this paper serve as examples of the kinds of tasks and issues that one must deal with as an Early Childhood Adviser to a television program for young children. There are many other areas to consider: the need in a predominantly visual program to balance active physical segments and those involving more looking and listening; how in the life-paced situation does one concentrate real time so that it also meets the requirement of good visual entertainment?; what techniques are valuable aids in stimulating and holding attention? There are also questions that might be explored for future directions. As children in the 1990's become more media literate, what levels of fantasy and visual "magic" can be sustained in a realistically-based program? Are there ways of incorporating more imaginative television techniques?

Pre-school children in the 1990's may not be so different from pre-school children in the 1970's in their essential approach to life. However, television is a constantly changing wonder and young children are surrounded by, and part of, a media-conscious culture. The best of that media world must be continually studied, harnessed and brought in touch with the world of the young child in a meaningful way. *Play School* has succeeded in this task to date. One hopes that children's programs with an equally high level of commitment and quality will continue to be made.

References

A.B.C. (1988) *Twenty One Years of Play School* (video). Recorded comments of unit personnel and actors. ABC: Sydney

A.B.C. (1970-1993) Play School program viewing reports and correspondence. Unpublished records: Play School unit: Australian Broadcasting Commission: Sydney

Anderson, D.R. & Lorch, E.P (1983) Looking at Television: Action or Reaction? in J. Bryant & D.R. Anderson (Eds). *Children's Understanding of Television*: Research on Attention & Comprehension. New York: Academic Press

De Vries, R. (1967) Conservation of general identity in the years three to six. Unpublished doctoral dissertation: University of Chicago

Donaldson, M. (1978) *Children's Minds*. Glasgow: Fontana/Collins

Dunn, G. (1977) *The Box in the Corner: Television and the Under fives*. University of East Anglia: John Libbey: IBA

Gardner, H. (1983) *Frames of the Mind: The theory of multiple intelligences*. Basic Books: New York

Greenman, J.T. (1991) Places for childhood in the 1990's. Proceedings of the 19th National Conference, Australian Early Childhood Association, Adelaide. Watson, ACT: Australian Early Childhood Association

Kendall, A. (1979) The impact of television on the developing child. National Conference Proceedings of the Australian Preschool Association, Sydney

Noble, G. (1979) Television and oracy: a psychological viewpoint. Unpublished paper presented at Developing Communication Competence in Children Conference, Armidale, September

Noble, G. & Duck, J.M. (1986) Children's attention to, and interactions with "Playschool". Preliminary analysis of viewing records. *Australian Journal of Early Childhood*, 11, 27-34

Noble, G. (1979-80) How children "use" Sesame Street and Playschool. *National Association of Australian University Colleges: 1979-80 Review*, 18-23

Stonehouse, A. (1991) Our Code of Ethics at Work. Resource booklet, No. 2. Canberra: Australian Early Childhood Association

Notes on contributors

SUZANNE DYER
Suzanne Dyer, Ph.D. is a lecturer in Movement and Health at the Institute of Early Childhood, Macquarie University, researcher of children's fitness and sports programs and of teacher attitudes towards physical education in early childhood.

KATHLYN GRIFFITH
Kathlyn Griffith is an early childhood specialist in children's literature and play and a doctoral candidate at Macquarie University, Sydney, NSW Australia.

URSULA KOLBE
Ursula Kolbe is currently the art director at the Child and Family Studies Centre, Macquarie University, a lecturer in visual arts at the Institute of Early Childhood an exhibiting artist and a free-lance film-maker.

HELEN MARTIN
Helen Martin is a tertiary educator and early childhood advisor to ABC TV, and director of the Children's Theatre and Drama School, Marion Street Theatre, Sydney, Australia.

JENNIFER NICHOLLS
Jennifer Nicholls lectures in Drama and Theatre Studies, is the Chair of PACT Youth Theatre, a member of the Drama Committee, Performing Arts Board of the Australia Council and the Chair of the Early Childhood Arts Unit, Macquarie University, NSW, Australia.

SUSAN ROBERTS
Susan Roberts, Ph.D. is a lecturer in media studies (film, photography and children's television) at the Institute of Early Childhood and a Master's candidate in clinical psychology at Macquarie University.

WENDY SCHILLER
Wendy Schiller, Ph.D. is Associate Professor of Early Childhood and the Convenor of Dance and the Child International Conference, Macquarie University (1994), a consultant to the Australian Gym Federation and Sports Commission and Children's Program Assessor for the Australian Broadcasting Authority.

CHRISTINE STEVENSON
Christine Stevenson lectures in Visual Arts, and is an inaugural member of the Rural Aboriginal Program committee at the Institute of Early Childhood, Macquarie University and Art Consultant for UNICEF, Australia.

LOUIE SUTHERS
Louie Suthers is a lecturer in early childhood music at Macquarie University, a music advisor for ABC TV's *Play School* program and Sydney Symphony Orchestra's Education Program, curriculum consultant to the New South Wales Department of School Education and a doctoral candidate at the Institute of Early Childhood, Macquarie University, Sydney.

ANN VEALE
Ann Veale, Senior Lecturer at the De Lissa Institute, University of South Australia coordinates the early childhood Masters program and lectures in Art and Music.

KATHLEEN WARREN
Kathleen Warren is a lecturer in Drama and Communication at the Institute of Early Childhood, author of the book *Hooked on Drama*, an adjudicator at the Sydney Drama Eisteddfods and a doctoral candidate at Macquarie University.

MARGARET WHITE
Margaret White is an ex-school principal, a lecturer in cognition and the arts at Macquarie University and Coordinator of an International Exhibition of children's art currently touring Australia and Europe.

DATE DUE